SUB-HIMALAYAN

A GRAMMAR OF THE KHASSI LANGUAGE

SUB-HIMALAYAN

A GRAMMAR OF THE KHASSI LANGUAGE

FOR THE USE OF SCHOOLS, NATIVE STUDENTS, OFFICERS AND ENGLISH RESIDENTS.

BY THE

REV. H. ROBERTS,

Formerly Head Master of the Cherrapoonjee Govt. Normal School; Author of the Anglo-Khssi Dictionary, and other Elementary Vernacular Books.

GYAN

Published by

Gyan Publishing House
5, Ansari Road
Daryaganj, New Delhi-110002
Phone: 011-47034999, 9811692060
E-mail: books@gyanbooks.com

Distribution Network
gyanbooks.com
India, USA, Canada, UK, Australia, France

ISBN : 978-81-212-4393-3 (PB)
First Published, 1891

2nd Impression 2020

Printed at: Gyan Press, Delhi.

A Grammar of the Khassi Language
Author: H. Roberts

SUB-HIMALAYAN.

A

GRAMMAR

OF THE

KHASSI LANGUAGE.

FOR THE USE OF SCHOOLS, NATIVE STUDENTS,

OFFICERS AND ENGLISH RESIDENTS.

BY THE

REV. H. ROBERTS,

Formerly Head Master of the Cherrapoonjee Govt. Normal School; Author of the Anglo-Khassi Dictionary, and other Elementary Vernacular Books.

LONDON:

KEGAN PAUL, TRENCH, TRÜBNER & CO., LTD.

PATERNOSTER HOUSE, CHARING CROSS ROAD.

1891.

DEDICATED

TO ALL MY OLD STUDENTS AND PUPILS

IN THE

KHASSI AND JAINTIA HILLS,

IN MEMORY OF THE PAST, AND AS A TOKEN OF MY CONCERN

FOR THEIR FUTURE MORAL AND INTELLECTUAL

ADVANCEMENT;

ALL, IN SHORT, THAT IS CONVEYED IN THAT BEAUTIFUL,

SUBLIME, AND COMPREHENSIVE WORD,

KHUBLEI!

THE AUTHOR.

CONTENTS.

III. Syntax.

INTRODUCTORY REMARKS.

THE importance which the Khassi and Jaintia Hills have of late years acquired, both as a frontier district and a centre of administration, will, I trust, amply justify the appearance of a complete and somewhat exhaustive Grammar of the language of by far the most numerous and powerful of the north-east frontier tribes. To those who, in the daily discharge of their official duties, come into personal contact with the natives, a practical knowledge of their language is indispensable. For it is *the* guide *par excellence* to a just appreciation of their character and habits. The numerous visitors from the extensive tea estates, to the salubrious and charming climate of the hill sanitarium at Shillong, now so easy of access from all parts, will also find in the Grammar a useful companion.

We would particularly call attention to two prominent features of the work:—1st, Complete paradigms for the conjugation of all Verbs, based on native usage, the *usus loquendi*, properly so called, have been supplied; 2nd, A detailed treatment of the Article;—subjects in regard to which the Khassi Language possesses features altogether its own, as compared with the other members of the Sub-Himalayan group.

By this means the Khassi youths (attending the Hill Schools), numbering some thousands, may be stimulated to greater diligence not only in acquiring a more systematic knowledge of their own language, but also in mastering the corresponding forms in English; as their prospects of obtaining more remunerative posts in the various Government departments, will mainly depend on their success in this last direction. The time is not far distant, no doubt, when a regular system of Competitive Examinations will be introduced into the Hills.

The Khassis and Taintias occupy a strip of mountain district between 70 and 90 miles in breadth, running east and west, having the Assam Valley for its northern boundary, and the Plain of Bengal, or Soormah Valley, for its southern. It is situate in the very centre of the Province of Assam—westward, as now constituted under a Chief Commissioner. The number of people speaking the language, under various modified forms, may be roughly estimated at 250,000.

In this work, the dialect of Cherrapoonjee is taken as the standard, because it is the purest, as universally acknowledged by the natives, besides being more amenable to systematical arrangement than the *patois* of the smaller villages. Such ugly barbarisms as *sngew* for *sngow*; *miew* for *miáw*; *sngoi* for *sngi*; *massoi* for *massi*; *kong* for *jing*; *lom* for *lúm*; *loi* for *leit*; *lïar* for *l'ér*; *ïam* for *ém*; *be* for *ém*; *pi lai* for *khie leit*; *how hai lëa* for *khie leit*; *kynang* for *tynga*; *loi-ar-keh* and *lëar ke* for *leit-kái; ham klam* and *ri shïar tha* for *wat kren*, and many others, should be avoided.

The principle of word-building, or agglutination, enters so largely and unavoidably into every section throughout the etymological portion of the Grammar, that a separate chapter on that subject is deemed unnecessary. A list of *foreign* importations from the Bengali and Hindustani, and *through* them from the Persian and Arabic, may not be without interest to a certain class; and would suggest a new method of mental training for the natives. Such a list, to be complete, would also contain a number of roots beyond all doubt identical in *form* with Hebrew roots bearing identical meanings. However strange this may at first appear, and without forgetting the usual caution of philologists, such erratic instances of distant affinity are not wanting; instances which the presence of Arabic words at second-hand will not always explain. Thus, صدق (*sadak*) is the Hebrew צֶדֶק (*tzedek*), and the Khassi *shida*, 'straight,' 'upright'; ناگ (*nág*) connects *naga*, 'a serpent,' with the Hebrew נָחָשׁ (*nakhash*). But no such connecting link is found for שֶׁקֶר (*sheker*) and the Khassi *shukor*, 'to deceive'; or between the Hebrew שֶׁרֶץ (*shere*) and the Khassi *shér*, 'a small fish,' or 'a *fry* of small fish'; or between נֵכָר (*nekar*) and *dykar* or *nykar* in *ki nykar*, 'strangers or foreigners.' The short time that is necessary to master the principles of this language will amply pay for the trouble.

The Khassis have no written language of their own,

and therefore no literature of any kind. There are no materials, so far as we know, from which to connect their present with the past, or to trace out a history for them. Although the country is studded with monolithic and cromlechian monuments, of immense size, reminding us of the Druidical remains of Stonehenge, Wales and Brittany, none of these bear inscriptions. Tradition, such as it is, connects them *politically* with the Burmese, to whose king, under the title of "Burm," they were up to a comparatively recent date rendering homage, by sending him an annual tribute in the shape of an axe, or *dáw*, as an emblem merely of submission.

Another tradition points out the north as the direction from which they migrated, and Sylhet as the *terminus* of their wanderings, from which they were ultimately driven back into their present hill fastnesses, by a great flood, after a more or less permanent and peaceful occupation of that district. The peculiarities of Sylhet Bengali, known as *The Sylheti*, so different from the more classical Bengali of Dacca and Calcutta, are attributable to this occupation; and the peculiar structure of the *Sylheti* lends some probability to the tradition. This entire absence of native literature, however, suggests a long period of isolation from the more civilized races; and to a certain class of thinkers it suggests a great deal more.

The Khassi Language is a member of that heterogeneous group, sometimes called the Sub-Himalayan, of which so little is known; too little to enable philologists to assign it any well-defined status in the large catalogue of languages which go to make up the Turanian family. The term Sub-Himalayan savours too much of the Great Adelung's long since abandoned system of classifying languages geographically. But whatever difficulties may still attend the attempt at a linguistic classification pure and simple, the *race* affinity of the Khassis to the surrounding Hill Tribes—Garos, Kookies, Nagas, Looshais, Munipoories &c., and even to the remoter Chinese, is unmistakeable. The Mongol physique in all its permanent features is established beyond doubt. While the racial affinity is evident, it is important however to state here, that the percentage of WORDS COMMON to the Khassi and the rest of these mountain dialects is extremely small; so small as to guarantee on *that* score no belief in their racial affinity. Equally great also is the dissimilarity in many other points of grammatical detail.

This apparent conflict between ethnology and language, so much insisted on now-a-days by a certain school of theorists, is nevertheless highly suggestive, and bespeaks a long period of isolation (of the Khassis) not only from some as yet unknown (perhaps undefinable) parent stock, but also from those tribes even which have for many centuries occupied districts contiguous to them.

What stage in *linguistic development* should we assign to the Khassi Language? We answer, that it is not so absolutely monosyllabic, like the Chinese on the one hand, as to be devoid of genuine agglutinations. On the other hand, it is too far removed from the so-called *inflexional stage* to be classed under the agglutinate family in the sense of *terminational;* for its agglutinations are in no sense *terminational* or *inflexional* as those terms are understood and handled by Professor Max Müller, to whom philology is so much indebted.

If the Professor's comprehensive definition of an agglutinate (*i.e.* Turanian) language is to be accepted as a final test or basis of classification, the Khassi is neither Turanian nor agglutinate. If we understand his definition rightly, it must be greatly modified to include the Khassi, and some of the other adjacent dialects within the extensive family, which his favourite term *Turanian* is intended to embrace. According to Prof. Max Müller,* it is a distinctive characteristic of a *Turanian* language, that it should be agglutinative, *not only* in the general sense of gluing its words, of having its words coalescing, but further, that the modifying root be *terminational,* and thus approach the higher stage of *inflexion.*

In the Khassi, however, the modifying roots even in agglutinates are *without exception* PREPOSITIVE. A very cursory perusal of the Grammar will substantiate our position. Take, e.g. *pyn* (from *pún,* 'to make'), or *pyl, pyd, pyr* in all Causative Verbs; *ia* of the Dative and Accusative; *ia* of Reciprocal Verbs; *la, la lah,* Past Auxiliaries; *yn* of the Future Tense; *jing* ('possession') of

* See Science of Language, vol. i. p. 323, fifth edition, 1866.

Abstract Nouns, and many other examples equally easy of comprehension; these are all *glued* and are all PREPOSITIVE. Here we have a language, on the north-east frontier of India, which has merged out of the purely monosyllabic stage, but which cannot be brought under the category of *terminational*, much less the *inflexional*, for it has no inflexions. Have we not here an example of an entirely new feature in the development of language? Any how, we cannot see the applicability of Prof. Max Müller's definition to the Khassi. Take, e.g., the root *lait*, 'free;' *-pyl-lait*, 'to make free;' *jing-pyl-lait*, 'freedom, or liberation.' The modifying roots move, as it were, backward, and not forward. Or can we detect here an *intermediate* stage between the purely monosyllabic and the terminational; or does this fact affect the validity of Prof. Max Müller's definition of a Turanian language?

But if we give the term *agglutinate* a less rigid acceptation, the Khassi Language could not be better described than in terms applied by a recent writer on Language to the Japanese*:—"It is an agglutinate dialect of extremely simple structure, with no determinate flexion, the relations of case [gender], number and person are indicated by separate particles [and] auxiliary words" [only let the student of Khassi bear in mind that these particles are PREPOSITIVE and not terminational]. "Combinations of separate root words with considerable contraction

* Whitney's Life and Growth of Language, p. 241. The words in brackets are our own.

and mutilation [or obscuration] is very common." Such, generally speaking, is the Khassi Language.

Examples of that peculiarity called *Harmonic Arrangement* or *Harmonic Sequence*, so common in other primitive forms of speech, are wanting; nor are there any duplications to form the plural; *phui-phui*, 'dust, dusty;' *phum-phum*, 'bushy;' *lat-lat*, 'rippling, in ripples, a ford;' *phàk phàk*, 'violently;' *ngur-ngur*, *ngèr-ngèr*, and many others, are onomatopœian or imitative, and intensive, rather than true plural forms.

Referring to onomatopœias, the *bow-wow* theory is strongly countenanced by the Khassi: *ksew* is 'a dog;' *kwack* is 'a duck;' *miáw* is 'a cat;' *ang* is 'to gape,' &c.

The next generation may see the Comparative Grammar, so much desired, giving an account of these numerous erratic boulders (to borrow the language of geology), and of their mutual relationship, if not of the parent stock from which they have been transported and scattered broadcast by force of events unknown. But special Grammars must first of all issue.

KHASSI GRAMMAR.

INTRODUCTION.

§ 1. GRAMMAR is the science which teaches how to speak and to write correctly in any language.

§ 2. Language (*Ka Ktín*) is composed of sentences, sentences of words, words of syllables, and syllables of letters; hence:—

§ 3. This Grammar is divided into three main parts, viz., (1) Orthography, or that which treats of the *letters* of the language; (2) Etymology, or that which treats of the various kinds of *words*, or *Parts of Speech;* and (3) Syntax (*Ka Jing-pyn-ia-ryn-tíh Ktín*), or that which teaches how words should be arranged into sentences, in order to express complete thoughts (*Ki Jingmùt*).

CHAPTER I.

Orthography.

§ 4. OF THE LETTERS.—The Khassi Alphabet consists of twenty-one letters only, viz.

A B K D E G NG H I J L M N
O P R S T U W Y

These letters are divided into three classes (*Lái jaid*), (1) *Vowels*, (2) *Semivowels*, and (3) *Consonants*.

§ 5. Of the Vowels (*Ki Dák Jur*).—The vowels are six in number, viz. *A, a; E, e; I, i; O, o; Y, y; U, u.**

These six vowels represent twelve simple sounds, five long and seven short; *two* are semivowels, and when combined form thirteen proper diphthongs.

§ 6. The twelve simple vowel-sounds may be thus exemplified:—

a short	like *a* in man;	as,	*tam*, too much;	*pat*, again.
á long	„ *a* „ far;	„	*bám*, to eat;	*dá*, to protect.
e short	„ *e* „ set;	„	*pep*, to fail;	*en*, to be quiet.
é long	„ *e* „ were;	„	*hér*, to fly;	*kér*, to enclose.
i short	„ *i* „ pit;	„	*tip*, to know;	*sim*, a bird.
í long	„ *ee* „ steep;	„	*íng*, a house;	*sím*, a king.
o short	„ *o* „ pot;	„	*lop*, to prune;	*sop*, to cover.
ó long	„ *o* „ go;	„	*óh*, to hew;	*ór*, to split.
u short	„ *u* „ put;	„	*lum*, to gather;	*sum*, to bathe.
ú long	„ *ao* „ boot;	„	*lúm*, a hill;	*súm*, to pierce.
y short	„ *u* „ fun;	„	*bynta*, a part;	*yn*, will.
y short	„ *y* „ Fr. *une*;	„	*synduk*, a box;	*shym*, not.

§ 7. The semivowels are:—

i, like *y* in 'yard;' as *iár*, 'to spread;' *iaid*, 'to walk:' or the য় in করিয়া (*kariyá*); as *iap*, 'to die;' *iuh*, 'to tread.'

w, like *w* in 'war;' as *wád*, 'to search;' *wan*, 'to come:' or ওয় in যাওয়া (*jáwá*);—

---

* The anomaly of including the *w* among the vowels should be done away with.

wir, 'astray;' *wang*, 'widely:' or ا, in پروانه (*parwána*): or *oi* in Fr. *avoir* (*av-wár*).

§ 8. The diphthongs are compound vowel-sounds, and may be exemplified thus:—

ai (short), like our vulgar 'ay;' as *pait*, 'to break:' or কাই in ডাকাইত (*dakait*); as *kait*, 'a plaintain.'

ái (long), like আয in কার্য্য (*káirja*); as *kái*, 'for pleasure:' or ائي in نایب (*náib*); as *lái*, 'three;' '*sái*, 'a thread.'

aw (short), like *äoo* in Fr. *aoûter*; as *law*, 'to take off:' or যাওয় in যাওয়া (*jawá*); as *kaw*, 'noisy:' or او in نواب (*nawáb*).

áw (long), like আওয় in পাওয়া (*páwá*); as *dáw*, 'a cause:' or Welsh *lláw*, 'hand;'—no English equivalent.

ei, like *ey* in 'they;' as *leit*, 'to go;' *peit*, 'to wake up;' *ngeit*, 'to believe;' not like *i* in 'thine,' as some foreigners pronounce it; but like এয় in জেয় (*jey*).

ew, like এও in দেওয়ানী (*dewaní*) or Welsh *tew*, 'fat'—no ex. in E—as *thew*, 'to measure;' *khew*, 'wheat.'

iw (short), like the '*u*' when simply pronounced; or یو in دیواني (*díwaní*); as *siw*, 'to pay;' *syntiw*, 'a flower.'

íw (long), like *eu* in 'feud,' or *u* in 'tune;' as *kíw*, 'to ascend.'

ie,—the nearest approach to a true digraph, but the sound of the *e* is perceptible; like the *e muet* in Fr., having a short guttural sound after the *i*;* as *ieh*, 'to let alone.'

oi (short), like *oi* in 'voice,' or *oy* in گويا *goyá*; as *soi*, 'to shave with an adze.'

ói (long), like *oy* in 'joy,' or অয় in ভয় *bhoy*; as *rói*, 'to increase.'

ui (short), like *oo+i*, or *ui* in Fr. *bruit*, and S. Wales *llwyd*, 'pale;' as *bùit*, 'skill.'

úi (long), like *ou-i* in Fr. *fouille*; as *túid*, 'to flow.'

§ 9. THE CONSONANTS.—The fourteen simple consonants present no difficulty. None of the intricacies of Oriental alphabets encounter the student here. The natives having no literature of any kind, a phonetic alphabet has been formed for them, and it meets all the requirements of the language.

The letter *g*, however, calls for a remark. All the words containing this letter are foreign importations, from and through the Bengali and Hindústaní, such as *gadda*, 'an ass;' *gora*, 'a white man;' *godam*, 'a store-room;' *gormi*, 'a kind of disease;' *guli*, 'a shot;' *gúda*, 'a swelling;' *gali*, 'abusive language;' *lagam*, 'a bridle;' and a few others.

---

* Those versed in French will, perhaps, remember Voltaire's remark on the *e* mute: "*Son qui subsiste encore après le mot commence, comme un clavecin qui resonne quand les doigts ne frappent plus les touches.*"—Dict. Philosophique.

§ 10. The imperceptible *h* is represented by an apostrophe (’), and somewhat similar in its power to the ۂ or ۃ of Persian and Hindústaní grammars, that is the هاي مختفي (*ha-i-mukh-tafi*), when it comes between two vowels and causes a hïatus, as in بہار (*be’ár*), as distinguished from بهار (*behár*). See Sir W. Jones’ Persian Grammar (Works, vol. v., 8vo, 1807). The same remark applies to the final *h* when preceded by a vowel, its power is that of a slight guttural; as *rah*, ‘to bear;’ *pah*, ‘to utter a sound;’ *lah*, ‘to be able.’

§ 11. *h* is never initial in Khassi before another consonant. Such combinations as *hl*, *hm*, *hn*, *ht*, *hp*, &c. are unknown, and, however barbarous a tribe may be, we doubt whether such combinations do at all represent actual sounds in any of its kindred dialects.

In the case of the Kookies, for instance, there is always an abrupt *y* sound, either preceding or intervening, the *h* serving as a kind of fulcrum. The Bengali হ্রী (*hrí*) is no exception.

§ 12. The Aspirated Letters.—These are *b*, *k*, *d*, *j*, *p*, *r*, *t*, *ng*, *s*. As in Bengali and Hindústaní, the *h* sound is merely *combined* or *added* to that of the preceding consonant, and not amalgamated *with* it; so differing materially from our English notion of an aspirated letter—e.g., *ph* do not make an *f*, but stand separate, as in ‘up-hill,’ without an hïatus.

bh, as *bhá*, pron. *b-há*, ‘good,’ = ভা or بها
kh, as *khá*, pron. *k-há*, ‘to give birth,’ = খা or كها

dh (ধ, دھ), as *dhah*, pron. *d-hah*, = 'a drum,' دھاہ
jh (ঝ, جھ), as *jhíh*, pron. *j-híh*, 'wet.'
ph (ফ, پھ), as *phuh*, pron. *p-huh*, 'to blossom.'
rh (*rh* in w-*rhwng*), as *rhem*, pron. *r-hem*, 'warm,' 'hot.'

Neither the Bengali nor the Hindústaní supply us with an equivalent. It is the Greek ῥ in ῥάβδος (*rhabdos*).

ngh, as in *rynghang*, pron. *ryng-hang*, 'ajar.'
th, as in 'beat-him' (থ, تھ), *tháw*, pron. *t-háw*, 'to make.'

sh is an exception; it is like *sh* in 'shine,' as *shong*, 'to stay:' the Bengali শ and Hindústaní ش, in শাপ and شاہ (*shah*), گوش (*gósh*).

§ 12. Orthographical Signs.—1. *The Accents.* (1) The *acute* (´), which marks the quantity of a vowel as long, as *dá*, 'to shield;' *bhá*, 'well.' (2) The *grave* (`), which is only occasionally employed, when the pronunciation is to be very abrupt; as *daìn*, 'to cut;' *kaìn*, 'very pointed' (to distinguish it from *'káin*, 'a fly'). (3) There is also a middle quantity which is perceptibly distinguished by the natives. These are vowels followed by *h* final; as *lah*, 'to be able;' *pah*, 'to cry;' *rih*, 'to rear.'

2. The *apostrophe* ('), to mark the suppression of one or more letters; as *'líng* for *khlíng*, 'a kite;' *'ping* for *sping*, 'a handle;' *'siw* for *ksiw*, 'a grandchild;' *'riw* for *briw*, 'a man or a human being;' *'rang* for *shinrang*, 'a male;' *thei* for *kynthei*, 'a female;' *ér* for *l'ér* or *lyer*, 'wind;' *'nám* for *snám*, 'blood;' *'súid* for *ksúid*, 'a demon;' &c.

Note.—Some of these are permanent elisions, while

most of them are *occasional*, and *euphonic;* e.g. a dæmon in *general* is always called '*ksúid;*' but when this is qualified by some descriptive word immediately following, to point out a particular kind of dæmon, the initial *k* is suppressed; as, *'súid-úm*, 'the water or fever dæmon.' This is an important point.

3. *The diærecis* (¨), placed above one of two contiguous vowels, in order to show that they are to be pronounced separately; as, *ïeit*, 'to love;' *bïeit*, 'foolish;' *rïam*, 'to ensnare;' *nïam*, 'religion;' *khaïi*, 'to trade;' *lïang*, 'side;' *rïai*, 'to sing.'

Note.—There are no true digraphs in Khassi. Each vowel should have its own separate sound. All the vowel combinations are *proper* diphthongs. This is owing to the fact of its being a language composed of root words; which, with a very few exceptions, are all used as independent words.

4. *The hyphen* (-) should be extensively used in order to show the formation of compounds, which in the majority of cases, are roots placed merely in juxtaposition to express *one compound idea.*

(1) Nouns *ár-ngut*, 'two persons,' 'a couple;' *ar-tylli*, 'two things, or two;' *san-shnong*, lit. 'five villages,' = a confederacy of five villages.

Note.—The emphasis is equally on both or each part of the compound.

(2) Verbs followed by a personal pronoun, as *leh-ma-phi*, 'you do.' (3) Verbs followed by an adverb, as *leh-bhá*, 'to do good;' *kam-sníw*, 'to do ill.' (4) Verbs

and Adjectives followed by *eh* (Fr. *très*), 'very,' as *kren-eh*, 'to speak harshly;' *bhá-eh*, 'very well.' (5) Verbs and pronouns followed by *hí* (Fr. *même*), 'self,' 'even;' as *ma-nga-hí*, 'I myself;' *wan-hi*, 'come yourself,' or 'come even.' (6) Nouns followed by demonstrative particles for the sake of emphasis; as *u briw-une* (instead of *une u briw*), 'this man;' *ka ing-hangne*, 'this here house,' or 'the house here.'

§ 13. Emphasis.—In pronouncing Khassi words, the emphasis should as a rule be on the penult, in the case of dissyllables; as *pynlong*, 'to cause to be;' *shítom*, 'trouble;' *pynwan*, 'to cause to come;' *jinglong*, 'a state;' *lynnong*, 'a part;' *kynsha*, 'desolate;' *hinrei*, 'but;' *dádín*, 'behind.'

There are many exceptions to this rule: (1) of words beginning with *pyn*, having the emphasis on the last syllable; as *pynjah'*, 'to loose;' *pynher'*, 'to fly,' (a kite); *pynhun'*, 'to soothe;' *pynsah'*, 'to leave behind;' *pynháp*, 'to let fall;' *pynong'*, 'to speak for another;' *pynum'*, 'to melt; *pynroi,'* 'to increase.' (2) With *ia*, as *iaroh'*, 'to praise;' *ialang'*, 'to gather together;' *iapom'*, 'to fight;' *iarap'*, 'to help;' *iaseng'*, 'to assemble;' in short, all words beginning with *ia* (prep.) should never have the emphasis on that prefix. In Shella and Jiwai, however, some of the natives violate this rule in some instances only, as *ia'rap*, instead of *iarap'*; but it is affected.

When a compound is made up of two or more dissyllable words, each retains its own emphasis; as *kyn'riah dádín*, 'to retire, to recede.'

When a dissyllable and a monosyllable form the compound, both retain their natural accent; as *hin'riw-phew*, 'sixty,' *hin'niew-phew'*, 'seventy;' *kyn'ruh-ktín'*, 'to rinse the mouth.'

Etymology.

§ 14. In the following eleven chapters we shall treat of the *Parts of Speech* in their usual order—*Article*, *Noun*, *Adjective*, *Pronoun*, *Verb*, *Adverb*, *Preposition*, *Conjunction*, and *Interjection*.

We should here remark that the Khassi Language is absolutely devoid of *inflection*, according to the strict sense of that word (see *Prefat. Remarks*). Some of the demonst. pronouns, and a few adverbs of place, do express different degrees of distance by a mere change of termination; as,

u*ne*, u*no*, u*ta*, u*tai*, u*to*.—Dem. Pronouns., which see.
sha*ne*, sha*no*, sha*ta*, sha*tai*, sha*to*.—Adverbs, which see

---

CHAPTER II.

The Article.

§ 15. There are four Articles in Khassi;—three in the singular, as *u* (masc.), *ka* (fem.), and *i* (dim. of both genders), and one in the plural for both genders, as *ki*.

u (masc.)
ka (fem.) for the singular, and } *ki*, the plural of all.
i (com.)

§ 16. Of the use of the Articles.—(1) They indicate the number and gender of nouns. This is the chief sense in which the article defines the noun in Khassi; as,

SINGULAR.	PLURAL.
u ksew, 'a *or* the dog.'	*ki ksew*.
ka ksew, 'a *or* the bitch.'	*ki ksew*, 'dogs *or* the dogs.'
i ksew, 'a *or* the little dog.'	*ki ksew*.

The rule is that one or other of the articles should be used before every noun, according to its gender, number, or importance. Nouns masculine take *u*, as *ubriw*, 'a *or* the man;' *u lúm*, 'a *or* the mountain;' *u máw*, 'a *or* the stone.' Nouns feminine take *ka*, as *ka díng*, 'a *or* the tree;' *ka ding*, 'a *or* the fire;' *ka sïang*, 'a *or* the spoon.' Diminutive nouns of either gender, or names of contemptible objects, take *i*; as *i briw*, 'a *or* the manikin;' *i khun-lung*, 'a *or* the baby.' All nouns in the plural should have *ki*; as *ki íng*, 'houses, *or* the houses;' *ki lúm*, 'mountains, *or* the mountains;' &c. (See §§ 19, 20.)

(2) It is the context only which determines whether these articles should be considered as definite or indefinite. There are no two sets of articles as in French (*un*, *une*; *la*, *le*), but only one, like the Greek ὁ, ἡ, τό). Ex.:—

1. Don *ki* sïar ha *ka* rú, 'There are *fowls* in *the* cage.'
   Ki sïar *ki* don ha *ka* rú, '*The* fowls are in *the* cage.'
2. *Ki* wïar ki ksew, '*The* dogs are barking.'

Note.—Here the word *wïar*, 'bark,' point to the species 'dogs;' hence the definite article *the*.

3. *Ki* ksew ki la háp ha úm, '*some* dogs fell into the water.'

Note.—The verb *háp* may apply to any other object; hence the definite article *the* is not specially required here.

CHAPTER III.

The Noun.

§ 17. The Noun is a name of anything we can see, feel, or think about; as *ka khún*, 'a daughter;' *u khún*, 'a son;' *ka jingmut*, 'a thought;' *ka jing bïeit*, 'imbecility;' *ki doh-khá*, 'fish,' or 'fishes;' *ka rong* (رنگ), 'colour.'

§ 18. In Khassi, as in English, there are three kinds of Nouns, viz. (1) *Common*, (2) *Proper*, and (3) *Abstract*.

(1) *Common Nouns* are names given to all objects of the same class (*kiba dei ia kajuh ka jáid*); as *ka massi*, 'a cow;' *u sim*, 'a bird;' *ka wah*, 'a river.'

(2) *Proper Nouns* are names given to one individual member of a class; as *Sohra*, 'Cherra;' *U Tirot*, 'Tirot' (the name of a well-known Khassi chief of Khad-sáw-phrá); *Ka Sunon*,* 'The goddess Sunon;' *Ka Sat*, 'The goddess Sat.'*

---

* From these two female deities the two most powerful chieftainships, Cherra and Shillong, are said to have descended.

(3) *Abstract Nouns* are the names of *states, actions,* and *qualities.* These are known chiefly by the prefix *jing-*; as,

ka jinglong, 'state;' from *long,* 'to be.'
ka jingiáp, 'death;' from *iáp,* 'to die.'
ka jingleh, 'action;' from *leh,* 'to do.'
ka jinghér, 'flight;' from *hér,* 'to fly.'
ka jingbïeit, 'foolishness;' from *bïeit,* 'foolish.'
ka jingkhá, 'birth;' from *khá,* 'to give birth.'

(*a*) Another way of forming *abstract nouns* is by prefixing the feminine article *ka* to adjectives, as the neuter τό is used in Greek, and *le* in French: τὸ πονῆρον, 'evil;' *l'infame,* 'infamy;' *le beau,* 'the beautiful;' *le sublime,* 'the sublime;' as—

ka babhá, 'the good;' from *babhá,* 'good.'
ka basníw, 'evil;' from *basníw,* 'bad.'
ka b'ymman, 'wickedness;' from *b'ymman,* 'wicked.'

Note.—These two forms cannot be used indiscriminately; the first corresponds to our abstracts in '-ness,' '-tion,' &c., and is more comprehensive; while the second is less emphatic, and corresponds to our verbals in '-ing,' when the root is a verb; as *ka jingleh,* 'action;' *ka baleh,* 'doing;' from *leh,* 'to do.'

(*b*) A few words express abstract ideas without either *jing* or *ba*; as—

ka tylang, 'the winter;' *ka dúr,* 'shape.'
ka pynïeng, 'height;' *ka pynkïang,* 'width.'
ka lyntér, 'length;' *ka thyma,* 'war.'

ka kam, 'occupation' (کام); *ka pop*, 'sin' (পাপ).
ka búit, 'talent;' (বুদ্ধি); *ka akor*, 'behaviour.'
ka nám, 'renown' (নাম); *ka dáw*, 'a cause.'
ka hok (حق), 'justice;' *ka bor*, 'power.'

(*c*) Some words, originally abstracts, have become common nouns; as *ka jing khang* (lit. a shutting) 'a door;' *ka jing sop* (lit. a covering) 'a roof;' *jing díe* (lit. a selling) 'merchandise, goods;' *ka jing thiah* (lit. a lying) 'a bed.'

(*d*) The form *ka*, with an adjective, is sometimes preferred merely for the sake of euphony, as more agreeable to the ear, and easier to pronounce; as—

(1) *Kabajing-ngái*, 'distance,' rarely *Ka jing jing-ngái*.
Ka bajing-ngái katno ha íng jong phi?
'What is the *distance* to your house?'

(2) *Kabajirhóh*, 'cough,' rather than *Ka jing-jirhoh*.
Kabajirhóh ka long ka dak ka ba sníw.
'*A cough* is a bad sign.'

(3) *Kabajingi*, 'swimming,' never *ka jing-jingi*.
U nang-eh ha *kabajingí*.
'He is clever at *swimming*.'

(*e*) Sometimes the natives drop off the adj. pref. *ba*, and prefix *ka* immediately to the root, to form abstracts; as—
ka shipá, 'difficulties;' *ka duk*, 'poverty;' *ka dukhá*, 'affliction.'
ka suk, 'happiness;' *ka sníw*, 'evil;' *ka jíwbór*, 'violence.' জবর or زبر.

These forms are used when a native aims at being eloquent; but *jing* is used when he is a careful and elegant speaker.

OF THE NUMBER OF NOUNS.

§ 19. The singular is formed by merely prefixing the singular article *u, ka,* or *i*; as, *u khlúr,* 'a star;' *u lúm,* 'a mountain;' *u kulái,* 'a horse;' *u lok,* 'a friend;' *ka kulái,* 'a mare;' *ka lok,* 'a female friend;' *i kulái,* 'a pony;' *i lok,* 'a little dear.'

The plural is formed by prefixing *ki,* the pl. of *u, ka, i* (§§ 15,16):—*ki kulai,* 'horses;' *ki lok,* 'friends;' *ki khlúr,* 'stars;' *ki lúm,* 'mountains.'

§ 20. THE PLURAL OF ANIMATE OBJECTS.—(1) As *ki* is the sign of the plural for both masculine and feminine nouns, we refer the student to the sections on Gender, especially § 28, Remark 5, where it is shown that a word indicating the gender is added; such as *shinrang,* 'male;' *kynthei,* 'female;' as—

> *ki 'lang-kynthei,* 'ewes,' or 'she-goats.'
> *ki 'lang-shinrang,* 'he-goats,' or 'rams.'

(2) In the same way with many diminutives; while the article *i* is sufficient in the singular to mark smallness, or endearment, some additional word or particle must be added in the plural; as—

> *i máw,* 'a pebble;' *ki máw*-ria, 'pebbles.'
> *i íng,* 'a little house;' pl. *ki íng*-rit, 'huts.'

i briw, 'a dwarf;' pl. *ki 'riw*-ráid, 'dwarfs.'
i sïar, 'a chicken;' pl. *ki* khún-*sïar*, 'chickens.'
i tynat, 'a sprig;' pl. *ki* 'nat-*rit*, 'sprigs.'

(3) In some cases the plural is formed by prefixing *ki* to a different word; as, *u briw*, 'a man,' pl. *ki 'rangbah*, 'men;' *ka briw*, 'a woman,' pl. *ki kynthei*, 'women.'

Note.—Strictly speaking, *ki briw* would mean 'human beings,' or men generally, male and female, in contradistinction to animals or things.

§ 21. Special facts:—(1) Some singulars either very seldom or never admit of a plural form; as—
ka snám, 'blood;' *ka doh*, 'flesh;' *ka jingduk*, 'poverty.'
ka sníh, 'poison;' *u sláp*, 'rain;' *u bynái*, 'the moon.'
ka sngi, 'the sun.'

(2) Some of the above, as well as a few others, take the plural, but with the meaning either greatly modified or entirely changed; as—

ka jingsarong, 'pride,' pl. *ki jingsarong*, 'airs.'
ka ksïar, 'gold,' pl. *ki ksïar*, 'gold ornaments.'
ka rupá (روپا), 'silver,' pl. *ki rupá*, 'silver ornaments.'
u sybái, 'money,' pl. *ki sybái*, 'shells,' 'cowries.'
ka kam (কাম, کام), 'work,' pl. *ki kam*, 'actions.'
u soh, 'fruit,' pl. *ki soh*, 'various fruits.'
u bynái, 'the moon,' (also a month), pl. *ki bynai*, months.
ka sngi, 'the sun,' pl. *ki sngi*, 'days.'
ka jingkhaïi, 'trade,' pl. *ki jingkhaïi*, 'goods.'
u sláp, 'rain,' pl. *ki slap*, 'the rainy season.'

kajingtháw, 'creation,' 'making;' pl. *kijingtháw*, 'ornaments.'

(3) Some singular forms have a plural meaning; as—

ka spah, 'riches;' *u soh*, 'fruit in general.'
u shniuh, 'hair;' *u shïap*, 'sand.'
u ksáin, 'grubs;' *u skáin*, 'flies.'
u krúin, 'white ants;' *u kybá*, 'grain.'
u krái, 'millet;' *u kháw*, 'rice.'
u phlang, 'grass;' *u sláp*, 'rain.'

Shnïuh, ksáin, skáin, shïap, kypá, kháw, sometimes take the diminutive article to express 'one hair,' 'one grain,' &c., as *i shnïuh, i shïap, i kháw, i kyba*, &c.

§ 22. Closely allied to those mentioned in last paragraph are the Collective Nouns; as—

ka kynhún, a flock, a herd; *u bynriw*, mankind;
ka jáid, a tribe, clan, or class; *u shnong*, a village community.
ka íng, (lit. a house), a family; *u paitbah*, the people.

Each of these are used in the plural with *ki* also; as *ki kynhún*, 'flocks;' *ki jáid*, 'tribes, or clans;' *ki íng*, 'families.'

§ 23. Some collectives are formed by joining two words, often (but not always) of a kindred meaning. These are double forms, and comprehend a certain class of things which go together in the ordinary routine of life or business. The words which form these collectives are names of objects or persons which suggest one another, either by way of contrast, or of similarity. It is a kind of

Hendyadis; as, *ka íng-ka sem,* (lit., 'a house and enclosure'), 'a house and appurtenances.'

ki khún-ki ksíw, (lit. 'children,' 'grandchildren')= posterity.

ka met-ka phád, 'the whole body.'

ka jainkúp-jain sem, 'clothes,' 'wearing apparel.'

ki jing buh-jing sah, 'furniture.'

ka jingbám-jing sá, 'food.'

ka shnong-ka'tháw, 'a king's subjects.'

u tymen-u san, 'the elders (of a village).

u rangbah-rangsan, 'the elders' (of a village).

ka jáid-ka skér, 'relatives.'

ka kot ka slá, 'documents, deeds.'

ka díng-ka síeit, (lit. wood, bamboo)=timber (for house building).

ka lúm-ka wah, (mountain-river, or valley), 'the whole country.'

ka lum-ka thor, 'highland and lowland.'

u ksúid-u khrei, 'dæmons.'

u shnong-u 'raid, 'the people,' and many others.

CASES OF NOUNS.

§ 24. Case shows the relation in which one Noun or Pronoun stands in respect to another Noun or Pronoun. In Khassi this relation is not expressed by any change in the *radical form* of either Noun or Pronoun, such as we find in Greek, Latin, or Bengali (see § 14), but by means of the prepositions *jong,* 'of;' *ha,* 'in,' 'to;' *ia,* 'to;' *na,* 'from,' &c.; and according to the strict grammatical import of the word, the Khassi language may be said to be without 'case.' The cases of other cultivated forms of speech may, however, be expressed in Khassi as follows:—

1. *Nominative*—The noun in its simple form; as,
U briw u la wan, 'The man came, *or* is come.'

2. *Accusative*—The noun in its simple form with and sometimes without *ia*. (See §§ 144, 145, 146.)
U la shem ia u briw, 'He found the man.'

3. *Dative* (*ba ái*), takes *ha*, or *ia*,* 'to;' as,
U la ái ha *nga ia ka kitab,* 'He gave *me* the book.'

4. *Instrumental*, takes *da* 'by;' as,
U la phot ia la ka ktí da *ka wait,* 'He cut his hand *with* an axe.'

5. *Ablative* (*ba mih na*), takes *na*, 'from;' as,
U Hom u la mih na la ing, 'Hom came *out* of his house.'

6. *Genitive*, also called the *Possessive* (*ba don*), takes the particle *jong*, 'of.' (See §§ 140, 141.)
Ka íng jong ka kymi, 'His mother's house.'

7. *Locative* (*ba dei jaka*), takes *ha* or *sha*, 'in, at, to;' as,
Ka kymi ka don ha ing, 'His mother is *at* home.'

8. *Vocative* (*ba khot*), takes *Ah!* or *Ko!* as,
Ah Blei! 'O God!' *Ko Kypá!* 'My *or* our Father!'

* The Chinese *yu* or *iu*.

Example:—*Briw*, 'man.'

	Singular.		Plural.
Nom.	*U briw*, a man.	N.	*Ki briw*, men.
Acc.	*Ia u briw*, a man.	A.	*Ia ki briw*, men.
Inst.	*Da u briw*, by a man.	I.	*Da ki briw*, by men.
Dat.	*Ha*, *sha*, or *ia u briw*, to *or* for a man.	D.	*Ha*, *sha*, or *ia ki briw*, to *or* for men.
Abl.	*Na u briw*, from a man.	A.	*Na ki briw*, from men.
Gen.	*Jong u briw*, of a man.	G.	*Jong ki briw*, of men.
Loc.	*Ha u briw*, with, in, *or* at a man.	L.	*Ha ki briw*, in *or* at men.
Voc.	*Ah briw!* O man! *Ko briw!* O my man!	V.	*Ah ki briw!* O men! *Ko ki briw!* O my men!

Note 1.—The preposition is often omitted (see § 141):

Ka íng ki briw, for *Ka íng jong ki briw*, lit. 'the house of (other) men,'=other people's house.

Wallam u briw, for *Wallam-ia u briw*, 'Bring a *or* the man.'

Note 2.—The article is also often omitted, both in the singular and the plural:

ai briw, for *ái ia u briw*, 'supply a man.'

ai briw, for *ái ia ki briw*, 'supply men.'

But see Syntax of *Articles* and *Prepositions*.

Gender of Nouns.

§ 25. Gender (লিঙ্গ) is the grammatical form by which we distinguish the sex (জাতি *játi*) of animated things.

In Khassi, as in French, all names, whether of animate or inanimate objects, are either masculine or feminine.

§ 26. These two genders are distinguished only by means of the articles *u*, *ka*, in the case of nouns singular; as—

ksew, dog, (male or female).
u ksew, a dog; *ka ksew*, a bitch.
briw, a human being.
u briw, a man; *ka briw*, a woman.
u sïar, a cock; *ka sïar*, a hen.
u trai, a master; *ka trai*, a mistress.
u snïang, a boar; *ka snïang*, a sow.

§ 27. There are cases (not numerous) in which the gender is known from the name, and then different words are used; as—

u kypa, a father; *ka kymi*, a mother.
u ktháw, a grandfather; *ka kïáw*, a grandmother.
u shinrang, a male; *ka kynthei*, a female.
u sír, a stag; *ka skei*, a deer.
u saheb, a gentleman; *ka mem*, a lady.
u kynráw, a bachelor; *ka 'thei-sotti*, a maid.
u rangbah, a man (adult); *ka kynthei*, a woman.

§ 28. In ordinary cases the plural with *ki* is common; hence some qualifying word indicating sex must be added, such as *shinrang* (male), *kynthei* (female); or a word describing some peculiar feature of the male, as *kyrtong* fat, strong) of cattle; *sohmoh*, or *soh-muh* (bearded), of goats; *bah* (big), of cocks.

ki sïar-bah, or *ki 'ïar-bah*, cocks.
ki massi, cattle; *ki massi-kyrtong*, bulls.
ki blang, goats; *ki 'lang soh-moh*, he-goats.
ki briw, men, people; *ki shinrang*, males.
ki ksew, dogs; *ki 'sew-shinrang*, male dogs.
ki 'sew-kynthei, bitches.
ki kulai, horses; *ki kulai-kynthei*, mares.

Note.—These qualifactory words are sometimes redundantly used in the *singular*, together with the article; as,

u 'kei-'rang, u skei shinrang, a buck.
ka massi-kynthei, a cow.
u massi-kyrtong, a bull.
u 'sew-shinrang, a male dog.

§ 29. The names of individual members of a class, when they take the article masculine (*u*), are of the *common* gender; as,

u briw, a human being; *u ksár*, a fox.
u sim, a bird (male or female); *u ksain*, a grub.
u khlá, a tiger (male or female); *u skáin*, a fly.
u 'nïang-bylliar, a lizard; *u risang*, a squirrel.
u 'nïang-bah ding, a glowworm; *u byshád*, a ferret.
u 'nïang-thoh-líh, leprosy; *u 'nïang-thyllíed*, thrush.
u 'kha-koi, a crab; *u 'khá-bysein*, the eel.

There are exceptions, as the names of most birds, which take the fem., *ka* :—

ka paro, a dove; *ka dykoh*, an owl.
ka tyngáb, a raven; *ka kybeit*, a hawk.
ka shapylloit, a lark; *ka tuta*, a parrot.

ka soh-lyngem, a wild pigeon; *ka khwak*, a vampire bat.
ka sarew, (সারশ) a crane; *ka lyngdykhur*, a pigeon.
ka pukni, a vulture; *ka khlíng*, an eagle.
ka hán হাস *hás*) a duck; *ka 'tid-'pú*, the cuckoo.
ka kyllai-toh-did, a wagtail; *ka ïar-tung*, the black pheasant.

Also some names of animals; as,

ka lyngtyna, a flying-squirrel; *ka jakoid*, a frog.
ka sharyntin, a weasle; *ka japhí*, a bull-frog.
ka hati, (হাতী *hatí*) an elephant; *ka miáw*, a cat.*

§ 30. When the species is particularly intended, the noun generally takes the feminine article *ka*; as,

ka ksew, the dog species; *ka díng*, wood (in general)
ka doh-khá, the fish kind; *ka máw*, stone (in general).

Another way of expressing the species or genus, very common in Khassi, is by using *kynja* (nature, kind) between the article and the noun; as, *ka kynja dokhá*, 'the fish kind:'

ka sim, or *ka kynja sim*, the bird kind, or species.

§ 31. Inanimate objects.—Practice only must be the guide here, but the majority by far are feminine:—

ka íng, a house; *ka líng*, a boat; *ka wah*, a river.
ka tari, a knife; *ka ding-duh*, a stick; *ka úm*, water.
ka sh'ing, a bone; *ka snám*, blood; *ka thied*, a nerve.

* The nouns under this section may be called *epicœne*, i.e. of one gender used for both sexes.

ka ktí, the hand; *ka khlíh*, the head; *ka rú*, a cage.
u lúm, mountain; *u máw*, a stone; *u soh*, a fruit.
u khwái, a hook; *u kwái*, the betel-nut; *u sping*, a haft.

§ 32. Abstract nouns are all feminine:—

ka jinglong, state; *ka jingpang*, pain; *ka jingduh*, loss.
ka hok, justice; *ka sut*, interest; *ka balut*, outlay.
ka kyán (ज्ञान), talent; *ka bor*, power; *ka jór*, essence.

Note.—The following *monadic nouns* are feminine; as, *ka sngi*, the sun; *ka pyrthei*, the world; *ka khyndew*, the earth; *ka duriáw*, the sea: but 'the moon' is masc., as, *u bynái*.

DIMINUTIVES.

§ 33. Under § 20, (2), we have already referred to the diminutives, which are formed by prefixing the article *i*; as, *i briw*, 'a little man,' or 'the iris;' *i hap*, 'baby.' Sometimes an additional word is placed either before or after the noun, both in the singular and plural, to suggest endearment, smallness, inferiority, or contempt; such as *khún*, lit. 'child;' *khynnah*, lit. 'child;' *rit*, 'small;' *rïa*, 'small;' as,

i máw-rïa, a pebble; *i sím-khynnah*, the king's heir.
i khún-blang, a kid; *i khún-bynriw*, a doll.
i khún-íng, a toy-house; *u saheb-khynnah*, a subordinate.
i íng, a hut; *i snïang*, a sucking-pig.

CHAPTER IV.

Of the Adjective.

§ 34. An Adjective expresses the quality (*ka jingiadei, ka jinglong*) of anything, and is in most cases distinguished by the prefix, or more properly the conjunctive particle *ba-* (lit. 'that,' conj.); as, *babhá*, 'good;' *bakhïa*, 'heavy;' *baeh*, 'hard;' *bakhïah*, 'healthy.'

Note.—There is no doubt but that this form of the adjective was originally an ellipsis; as, *ba+bhá*='that (is) good.'

u bríw babhá, lit. 'a man that (is) good'=a good man.

§ 35. The adjective, however, often rejects the prefix *ba*; as,

u 'ríw-sníw, a bad man; *u 'ríw-rúnar*, a cruel man.
u 'ríw-khúid, a pious man; *u 'ríw-bymman*, a wicked man.
ka íng-khráw, a large house; *ka lyér-khrëat*, cold wind.

Note 1.—This is probably the original form (without *ba*) of the adjective; and we reject the opinion that the adjective is formed from adverbs with *ba*. For there are many adverbs now in use which cannot take *ba* alone to form adjectives; such as, *ryngmang*, suddenly; *makynna*, aimlessly, triflingly; *kyndong*, aside; *ngain*, very; *sïar*, slily; *kyndit*, suddenly;—*baryngmang*, *bamakynna*, *bakyndong*, *basïar*, *ba kyndit*, are not admissible as simple adjectives.

Note 2.—When the adjective is thus used in its simple form, without *ba*, it often differs in meaning from the same adjective when used with *ba*; as,

u bríw-babhá	= a good man.
u 'ríw-bhá	= a rich man.
u bríw-bastád	= a learned man.
u 'ríw-stád	= an astrologer.
u soh-baiong	= a black fruit.
u soh-iong	= a plum (black).
u bríw-baiong	= a black or dark man.
u ríw-iong	= a negro.
u ríw-babïeit	= a foolish man.
u 'ríw-bïeit	= an idiot.
ka íng-barit	= a small house.
ka íng-rit	= a hut, an appurtenance.
ka íng-bakhráw	= a large or big house.
ka íng-bah	= the big or principal house (of the village).
u sím u balíh	= a king (who is) white, or a white man.
u sím líh	= One of the Khassi Chieftains of a particular district, always called 'The white chief.'

The first of the above double forms is merely descriptive, but the second refers to a definite class of objects with certain permanent attributes. This explains the fact that some adjectives are always without both the article and the prefix *ba*, as *u ksew-lamwir*, 'a mad dog.' The natives, though ignorant of the principles of Grammar, never violate this rule.

Note. 3.—The article may be repeated or omitted before the adjective; as, *ka íng bakhráw*, or *ka íng ka bakhraw*, 'a large house;' *u sniang basngáid*, or *u sniang u basngáid*, 'a fat pig;' *ka wah bajilliw*, or *ka wah ka bajilliw*, 'a deep river.'

Note 4.—From the above examples it will be seen that the adjective follows the noun it qualifies. When the adjective appears to go before the noun, the phrase becomes virtually an assertion; as,

ba íhsih u briw = because the man is hateful or ugly.
u ba ihsih u briw = the man is hateful or ugly. (See Syntax, § 110, note.

§ 36. *Other parts of speech* are used in compounds as adjectives: (1) Nouns; as,

ka dew-met=*dew*, earth+*met*, body=ashes.
ka doh-met=*doh*, flesh+*met*=lean flesh.
ka doh-khlein=*doh*, flesh+*khlein*, fat=fat.
ka dúr-briw, = *dúr*, shape, + *briw*, man or human, = portrait.
u soh-phlang, = *soh*, fruit, + *phlang*, grass, = earth-nut.
i 'lang-khún=*'lang*, a goat+*khún*, child=a kid.

The following are examples of nouns qualifying adjectives:

ba jerong-ktí=*ba jerong*, long+*ktí*, hand=long-handed.
ba sníw-briw = *basníw*, ugly+*briw*, person= ugly, unhandsome.
ba rit-jingmut = *barit*, small + *jingmut*, mind = small minded.

bakhráw-tyngám=*bakhraw*,large+*tyngám*, jaw,=noisy, talkative.

(2) Verbs; as,

doh-iáp=*doh*, flesh+*iáp*, to die=mortified flesh.

ka kot-pynhér=*kot*, paper+*pynher*, to fly=a paper kite.

dew-long=*dew*, earth, soil+*long*, to be=solid ground, original soil.

dew-roh=*dew*, earth+*'roh*, to deposit=alluvium.

u massi-dáb = *u massi*, an ox+*dáb*, to castrate = a gelded ox.

u sim-pyrthuh=*sim*, a bird+*pyrthuh*, to imitate=the mocking-bird.

§ 37. Gender of Adjectives.—The gender of adjectives is known from the article prefixed, which is that of the noun qualified; as, *ka dawái ka babhá*, 'good medicine.' Or, when the article is omitted, from the noun itself; as, *ka dawái babhá*, 'good medicine;' *u khlá ba rúnar*, 'a fierce tiger.'

§ 38. The Comparison of Adjectives.—The Comparative is formed, (1) by prefixing the adverb *kham* (more) to the adjective in its simple form; as—

Positive.	Comparative.
baeh, hard;	*ba kham eh*, harder.
baiong, black;	*ba kham iong*, blacker.
barit, small;	*ba khum rit*, smaller.
basan, tall;	*ba kham san*, taller.
basngáp, silentious;	*ba kham sngáp*, more taciturn.
baheh, big.	*ba kham heh*, bigger.

(2) Another mode of comparison is by using the simple adjective, with a noun or pronoun in the oblique case, with *ia*; as—

Ia kane, bha kato, lit. 'than this, good that,'=that is *better* than this.'

Ia *ka blang,* bhá *ka massi ba'n ái dùd,* 'the cow is *better than* the goat for giving milk.'

The Superlative is formed, (*a*) by adding *tam* (lit. 'to exceed') to the positive; as, *babhá,* 'good;' *babhá tam,* 'best.' (*b*) By adding *tam* to the comparative—*ba kham bhá,* 'better;' *ba kham bhá tam,* 'best.' (*c*) By adding *kham tam* to the positive; as, *babhá kham tam,* 'best, most good.' (*d*) By using the simple adjective with a noun in an oblique case, or a prep. phrase, like the Bengali (see Syntax, § 169); as, *na kine bhá katai,* lit. 'of these, good that,'=that is the best. (*e*) The superlative absolute [in which any quality or state is set forth in its highest or lowest possible degree] is expressed by adding the particle *eh* (very, &c.), or *shikkadei eh,* to either the positive or the superlative; as—

(1) To the Positive:

ba rúnar eh,
ba rúnar shikkadei eh, } most exceedingly cruel.

(2) To the Superlative:

ba rúnar tam eh,
ba rúnar kham-tam-eh, } most cruel.

ba runar tam-shikkadei,
ba runar tam-shikkadei eh, } most exceedingly cruel.

EXAMPLES (*Recapitulation*).

	Posit.	Comp.	Superl.	
1.	*barit,* (small)	*ba kham rit,* (smaller)	*ba kham rit-tam,* *ba rit kham-tam,* *ba rit-tam,*	(smallest).
2.	*ba heh,* (big)	*ba kham heh,* (bigger)	*ba heh tam,* *ba kham-heh-tam,*	(biggest).
3.	*baeh,* (hard)	*ba kham eh,* (harder)	*baeh tam,* *ba kham-eh-tam,* *baeh kham-tam,*	(hardest).
4.	*basníw,* (bad)	*ba kham sníw,* (worse)	*basníw-tam,* *ba kham-sníw-tam,* *ba sníw-kham-tam,*	(worst).

REMARKS.

1. *Kham* is often used in the sense of 'rather,' or of the English suffix '-ish;' as—

u kham *rúnar,* he is *rather* cruel.

u kham *sníw,* he is *rather* bad.

u kham *bhá u briw,* he is *rather* a good man.

u kham *sníw u briw,* he is *rather* a wicked man.

(2) *Eh,* besides as a sign of the superlative absolute, this particle has often the signification of 'too;' as—

Shim ia kane. *Em, ba ka sníw* eh.

Take this. No, for it is *too* bad.

(3) *Tam*—which is probably the Bengali superlative suffix তম (*tam*), still used (in Khassi) as an independent word, জ্ঞানী তম (*gani-tam*) = *kyán-tam* in Khassi, 'wisest'—often means 'more,' or 'over;' as, *Phi la ai tám,* 'You have given (something) *over;*' *Tó ái tam ho?* 'Give *more,*

will you?'—and also 'too much,' as, *Phi la ái* tam, may mean 'You have given *too much.*'

§ 39. The following are exceptions to the foregoing rules:

(1) Some few are compared irregularly, as in reckoning family precedence according to age—

ba dang khynnah,	*ba kham hadín,*	*ba khadduh.*
(young)	(younger)	(youngest).
ba la san,	*ba la kham san,*	*ba nyngkong,* or
(old)	(older)	*ba shiwa eh,*
		(eldest).

'Old' and 'young' in general are regular—

ba rim,	*bakham rim,* &c.
(old)	(older).

(2) Some adjectives which express the possession of a quality in a small degree, and begin with *byr* (our '-ish'), rarely admit of comparison; as, *byr'tem* (*byrstem*), yellowish; *byrsáw,* reddish; *byrthïang,* sweetish, mellow; *byrjew,* sourish; *byriong,* blackish; *byrlih,* whitish; *byrngut,* darkish, indistinct; *byrngïa'ng,* bitterish; *byrthuh,* greyish; *byrshem,* to abut; &c.

Numeral Adjectives.

§ 40. Numbers are either Cardinal or Ordinal.

(1) *Of the Cardinal Numbers.*—These are the chief or principal numbers, and they state 'how many,' or 'how much,' (*katno?*). We shall give as many examples here as

will enable the student to master this portion of Khassi Grammar :—

1. *shi,* or *wei* (com.), 'one;' and *uwei* (masc.), *kawei* (fem.), 'one.'

2. *ár,* two.	11. *khad-wei,* eleven.
3. *lái,* three.	12. *khad-ár,* twelve.
4. *sáw,* four.	13. *khad-lái,* thirteen.
5. *san,* five.	14. *khad-sáw,* fourteen.
6. *hinriw,* six.	15. *khad-san,* fifteen.
7. *hinniew,* seven.	16. *khad-hinriw,* sixteen.
8. *phrá,* eight.	17. *khad-hinniew,* seventeen.
9. *khyndái,* nine.	18. *khad-phrá,* eighteen.
10. SHI-PHEW, ten.	19. *khad-khyndái,* nineteen.

20. ÁR-PHEW, twenty (lit. two-tens).

21. *ár-phew-wei,* twenty-one.
22. *ár-phew-ár,* twenty-two.
23. *ár-phew-lái,* twenty-three.
24. *ár-phew-sáw,* twenty-four.
25. *ár-phew-san,* twenty-five.
26. *ár-phew-hinriw,* twenty-six.
27. *ár-phew-hinniew,* twenty-seven.
28. *ár-phew-phrá,* twenty-eight.*
29. *ár-phew-khyndár,* twenty-nine.†

30. LAI-PHEW = three tens, or thirty.

31. *lái-phew-wei,* thirty-one.
32. *lái-phew-ár,* thirty-two.

* 28 is also expressed thus, *lai-phew-'nár.* } See note 1.
† 29 „ „ *lai-phew-'nawei.* }

33. *lái-phew-lái,* thirty-three.
34. *lái-phew-sáw,* thirty-four.
35. *lái-phew-san,* thirty-five.
36. *lái-phew-hinriw,* thirty-six, &c.

40. SÁW-PHEW=four tens, or forty.

41. *sáw-phew-wei,* forty-one.
42. *sáw-phew-ár,* forty-two, &c.

50. SAN-PHEW=five tens, or fifty.

51. *san-phew-wei,* fifty-one.
52. *san-phew-ár,* fifty-two.
53. *san-phew-lái,* fifty-three.
58. *san-phew-phrá,* fifty-eight, or *hinriw-phew-'nár,* lit. six tens less two.
59. *san-phew-khyndái,* fifty-nine, or *hinriw-phew-'nawei,* lit. six tens less one.
60. *hinriw-phsw,* six tens, or sixty.
70. *hinniew-phew,* seven tens, or seventy.
80. *phrá-phew,* eight tens, or eighty.
90. *khyndái-phew,* nine tens, or ninety.
100. *shi-spah,* one hundred.
101. *shi-spah-wei,* one hundred and one.
200. *ár-spah,* two hundred.
300. *lái-spah,* three hundred, &c.
900. *kyndái-spah,* nine hundred.
999. *khyndái-spah-khyndái-phew-khyndai,* nine hundred ninety-nine.

The principle of *gluing* together, or of collocating the simpler to form the more complex numbers, is so steady and so regular, that they require only a little practice and repetition to master.

1000. *hajár*, one 'thousand.'

This is a foreign importation from the Persian هزار *hazár*, through the Bengali হাজার *hajár*. They have not utterly rejected their own *shiphew-spah*, lit. one-ten-hundred.

Note 1.—Any multiple of ten minus one, or minus two is often expressed thus:

18=*ár-phew-'nar*, contr. fr. *ár-phew-duna-ár*=two tens-less-two=eighteen.

19=*ár-phew-'nawei*, contr. fr. *ár-phew-dúna-wei* =two-tens-less-one=nineteen.

28=*lái-phew-'nár*, contr. fr. *lái-phew-dúna-ár* =three-tens-less-two=twenty-eight.

29=*lai-phew-'nawei*, contr. fr. *lai-phew-dúna-wei* =three-tens-less-one=twenty-nine.

Note 2.—The original force of *khad*, *phew* and *spah*, which continually recur, may be ascertained either from their use as independent words, or from analogy.

(1) *Khad* was in an earlier stage *the* word for 'ten.' The examples under Note 1 show that *khyndái* (nine) is a contraction of *khad-dúna-wei* or *khyndai*=ten-less-one; hence *khad-wei*=ten-one=eleven, &c., &c.

(2) *Phew*. As 'seven' was with the Hebrews, so is 'ten' with the Khassis, their 'perfect' or 'sacred' number. In one instance only do we find *khad* employed thus, viz. in the compound *shi-khad-dei*, 'a great deal.' But now we hear *shi-phew-jaid*, *shi-phew-rukom*, 'ten kinds or ways,'

i.e. 'many kinds,' &c.; also *ka spah-ka* PHEW, for 'abundance of wealth.'

(3) *Spah* is undoubtedly a contraction of *shiphew-shiphew*=ten times ten; and is by metonomy used for 'wealth,' *ka spah*.

Note 3.—*Shi* (one) more properly conveys the idea of unity, or oneness: *shi-sngi*, 'a whole day;' *shi-tylli*, 'a whole' of anything; *shi-íng*, not only 'one house,' but also 'a whole house or family;' *shi-shnong*, 'the whole village.'

100,000. *shi lak*, 'one lac'=one hundred thousand, from the Bengali লাক, or Sanskrit (Hind. لاکه), *lákh*.

shi khlúr means to a Khassi, a countless number; hence the stars are called *ki khlúr*: may be, this is the Urdu کرور *kurór*.

Collective Numbers.

§ 41. *shi-gynda* (Bengali গণ্ডা), گنڈا *ganda*, one anna of four pice, or four.

shi-gynda-kawei, one anna one pice, or five.

shi-gynda ár shíng, one anna two pice, or six.

shi-gynda lái shíng, one anna three pice, or seven.

ár-gynda, a two-anna piece, or eight pice.

lái-gynda, three annas, or twelve pice.

sáw-gynda, four annas, or sixteen pice.

sáw-gynda ár-shíng, four annas two pice, or eighteen.

sáw-gynda is also called *shi-suka*, or the four-anna piece (Bengali সিকি).
san-gynda, five annas, or twenty pice.
hinriw-gynda, six annas, or twenty-four pice.
hinniew-gynda, seven annas, or twenty-seven pice.
hinniew-gynda-lái-shíng, seven annas, threepice.

Instead of *phrá-gynda*, for 'eight annas,' they use *shi-phïah*, lit. 'one split or half,' *i.e.* eight annas, or one half-rupee, or sixteen annas; *lái-suka*, 'three fours,' or twelve annas; *shi-tyngka*, 'one rupee.'

Note.—The above are used chiefly in money computations, though the first, *gynda*, is used also in other reckonings.

shi-bydí, twenty, or a score; sometimes *shi kuri*, کوري.
shi-bydi-ar-gynda=twenty-eight.
shi-bydí-lái-gynda=thirty-two.
ár-bydi=two scores.
lái-bydi=three scores.

SHI-PÉN (পন)=eighty, or four scores.
ár-pén=two eighties, or 160.
lái-pén=three eighties, or 240.
saw-pén=four eighties, or 320.

SHI-KÁW (কাহন)=sixteen eighties, or 1280.
ár-káw=thirty-two eighties, or 2560.

Note.—These are used in counting bamboos and oranges; *e. g.* bamboos are sold by the fours (*gyndas*), or the scores (*bydi*), or four scores (*pén*).

§ 42. Ordinals.

These are formed by prefixing *ba* to the numerals, with the exception of 'first,' which has a separate word; thus—

1st. *nyngkong*, or *ba nyngkong*, first.
2nd. *ba ár*, second.
3rd. *ba lái*, third.
4th. *ba sáw*, fourth.
5th. *ba san*, fifth; &c.

Ex. *Une u long u* ba-lái *ba'n wan shane*, 'this is the *third* to come here.'

U la jïa long u ba nyngkong, 'he happened to be the *first*.'

§ 43. *The Reduplicative Numerals.*—(1) To express time, or our 'times.' These are formed by adding *wád* or *sin* (times) to the cardinal numbers; as—

shi-wád, or *shi-sín*, once.
ár-wád, or *ár-sín*, twice.
lái-wád, or *lái-sín*, thrice.
sáw-wád, or *sáw-sín*, four times; &c.

From these are formed the multiplicatives; thus—
ar-sín-ár = 'twice two;' *lái-sín-sáw*, 'three times four;' &c.

(2) To express quantity (*shah* = -fold) by adding *shah* to the cardinal numbers; as—

ár-shah, 'two-fold;' *sáw-shah*, 'four-fold.'
lái-shah, 'three-fold;' *shiphew-shah*, 'ten-fold.'

§ 44. *The Distributive Numerals.*—These are formed by merely repeating the cardinals; as—

ár-ár, 'by twos;' *sáw-sáw*, 'by fours.'
lái-lái, 'by threes;' *san-san*, 'by fives.'

Or by prefixing *mar* (each); as—

mar-kawei-kawei, 'one each,' or 'one by one.'
mar-wei-wei, 'one by one.'
mar-ár-ár, 'two each,' or 'by twos.'
mar-lái, 'three each,' or 'by threes.'
mar-phrá-phrá, 'eight each,' or 'by eights.'

§ 45. *Fractional Numbers*:—

shi-pawa, (پاو *páo*), a quarter; or *kaba sáw-bynta*, the fourth part.
shi-teng (lit. one part), a half; or *kaba shi bynta*, the one part.
ka ba lai bynta, the one-third.
shiteng páwa, the one-eighth, or *ka ba phrá-bynta.*
lái-páwa, three quarters.
shi-tyngka-phïah, one rupee and a half.
ár-phïah, two rupees and a half.
lái-phïah, three rupees and a half.

§ 46. *Measures*:—

shi-kham, a hand-breadth=four inches.
shi-tydah, a span=nine inches.
shi-prúh, a cubit=eighteen inches.
shi-kot, two cubits=thirty-six inches=a yard.
shi-kyntin-kwái=a mile (*sic*), or the space a man at his usual pace traverses, while chewing one-fourth of a betel-nut.

CHAPTER IV.

Pronouns.

§ 47. The Pronouns are of three kinds, viz. Personal, Relative, and Adjective.

§ 48. The Personal Pronouns are—1st pers., *nga*, 'I;' pl. *ngi*, 'we;'—2nd pers., *me* (masc.), *phá* (fem.), 'thou;' pl. *phi*, 'you;'—3rd pers., *u* (masc.), 'he' or 'it,' *ka* (fem.), 'she' or 'it;' pl. *ki*, 'they;' *i* (dim. masc. or fem.), 'he,' 'she,' or 'it.'

Personal Pronouns Declined.

1st Person—*Ngá*, 'I.'

Singular.	Plural.
N. *nga*,* 'I.'	N. *ngi*, or *ma ngi*, 'we.'
A. *ia nga*, 'me.'	A. *ia ngi*, 'us.'
I. *da nga*, 'by me.'	I. *da ngi*, 'by us.'
D. *ia* or *ha nga*, 'to me.'	D. *ia* or *ha ngi*, 'to us.'
Ab. *na nga*, 'from me.'	Ab. *na ngi*, 'from us.'
Gen. *jong nga*, 'of me or my, mine.'	Gen. *jong ngí*, 'of us, our, or ours.'
Loc. *ha* or *sha nga*, 'at, with, or in me.'	Loc. *ha* or *sha ngi*, 'at, with, or in us.'
Voc. *Ah ma-nga!* 'Ah me!'	Voc. *Ah ngi!* 'Ah we!'

Note.—In the valleys to the west, and in Jaintia to the east, *ma-i*, *ia-i*, *na-i*, 'I, me, from me,' are used. For the use of *ma-* before the pers. pronoun, see Syntax.

Note.—The locative *ha nga*, *sha nga*, &c., in all the pers. pronouns, is equal to the French *chez moi*, *chez nous*, &c.

---

* The Chinese *ngo*.

2nd Personal Pronoun.

Singular.	Plural.
N. *mé*, or *ma-mé* (m.), *phá*, or *ma-phá* (f.), 'thou.'	N. *phi* or *ma-phi*, 'you.'
A. *ia mé* (m.), *ia phá* (f.), 'thee.'	A. *ia phi*, 'you.'
I. *da mé* (m.), *da phá* (f.), 'by thee.'	I. *da phi*, 'by you.'
D. *ia* or *ha mé* (m.), *ia* or *ha phá* (f.), 'to thee.'	D. *ia* or *ha phi*, 'to you.'
Ab. *na mé* (m.), *na phá* (f.), 'from thee.'	Ab. *na phi*, 'from you.'
Gen. *jong me* (m.), *jong phá* (f.), 'of thee, thine, thy.'	Gen. *jong phi*, 'your,' &c.
Loc. *ha* or *sha me* (m.), *ha* or *sha pha* (f.), 'in, at, or with thee.'	Loc. *ha* or *sha phi*, 'in, at, or with you.'
Voc. *Ah me!* (m.), *Ah pha!* (f.), 'Oh thou!'	Voc. *Ah phi!* 'Oh ye!'

Note.—*Mé*, *phá*, like the French *tu*, are used between intimate friends, members of a family, or by a superior to an inferior person. *Ma-phi*, like the English 'you,' is used in addressing a single individual.

3rd Personal Pronoun.

Singular.	Plural.
N. *u*, *ka*, 'he, she, it.'	N. *ki*, or *ma-ki*, 'they'
A. *ia u* (m.), 'him, it;' *ia ka* (f.), 'her, it.'	A. *ia ki*, 'them.'

Singular.	Plural.
I. *da u* (m.), 'by him or it;' *da ka* (f.), 'by her or it.'	I. *da ki*, 'by them.'
D. *ia* or *ha u* (m.), 'to him, &c.; *ia* or *ha ka*, (f.), 'to her,' &c.	D. *ia* or *ha ki*, 'to them.'
Ab. *na u*, (m.), 'from him,' &c.; *na ka* (f.), 'from her,' &c.	Ab. *na ki*, 'from them.'
Gen. *jong u* (m.), 'his, or its;' *jong ka* (f.), 'her or its.'	Gen. *jong ki*, 'their, theirs.'
Loc. *ha* or *sha u* (m.), *ha* or *sha ka* (f.), 'in, at, or with him,' &c.	Loc. *ha*, or *sha ki*, 'in, at or with them.'

Note. 1.—It will be seen from the above that the 3rd personal pronoun is the article *u, ka, ki*, used alone.

Note 2.—*Ma-* should be used only in the nominative and vocative cases, only before the pers. pronoun, and never after any of the prepositions. Such forms as *ia ma-u, ia ma-nga, da ma-u*, are seldom heard. It is used, however, after the conjunction *bad* (and), as *bad ma-nga, bad ma-mé, bad ma-phí, bad ma-u*, &c.; when *bad* = 'with,' the *ma-* is dropped.

Note 3.—*Ki* (pl.) is often used honorifically for the singular *u*, or *ka*.

The emphatic Personal Pronoun.

1. The emphatic pers. pronoun is formed by adding *hí*, which is our English 'self,' Bengali আপনি, Hindustani آپ, Lat. *-pse -met;* as,

   U-hí or *ma-u-hí*, He himself.

   Mé-hí or *ma-mé-hí*, Thou thyself.

   Ngá-hí or *ma-nga hí*, I myself.

   For the force of *ma-* and *hí*, see Syntax, §§ 188, 197.

2. Sometimes *lade* is used with or without *hí*; thus,

nga lade,	*ma-nga lade.*
nga lade hí,	*ma-nga lade hí.*

   But besides emphasis, *lade* adds the subordinate notion of 'alone,' or 'of one's own accord,' as is sometimes the case with our English 'self:'

   Nga hí, nga'n leit, I will go myself.

   Nga lade hi nga'n leit, I will go myself.

   Nga'n leit lade hí, I will go myself.

3. *Hí*, 'self,' may be joined to any case of the noun or pronoun. See Note 2, above.

Relative Pronouns.

§ 49. The Relative is formed by using the conjunctive particle *ba* (that) after, or as a suffix to the article (used as a pers. pronoun). It is this *ba* which constitutes the relation with some antecedent. From the Syntax it will be observed, that the article is always repeated before the verb, to represent the subject, and to connect the subject with its predicate. In the same way it is often repeated before adjectives, or qualificatory clauses. As the adjective almost always requires *ba* to connect it with the noun, so in many cases the *ba* gradually becomes detached from the adjective itself and more intimately joined to the article, and thus forms the Khassi relative:

u briw u basníw = 'a bad man.'
u briw uba sníw = 'a man who (is) bad.'

(See Syntax, §§ 188, 189.)

§ 50. The relative pronouns are, according to the number of the articles, *uba* (masc.), *kaba* (fem.), *iba* (dim. m. and f.), 'who, which, that,'—pl. of all, *kiba*. Read carefully § 198, where it is explained how these forms may in the strictest sense be considered as both antecedents and relatives.

§ 51. The Relatives are declined in the same way as the simple personal pronouns :—

Singular.	Plural.
N. *uba* (masc.), *kaba* (fem.) *iba* (dim.), 'who,' &c.	N. *kiba*, 'who.' (for all genders.)
A. *ia uba* (masc.), *ia kaba* (fem.), *ia iba* (dim.), 'whom,' &c.	A. *ia kiba*, 'whom.' (for all genders.)
I. *da uba*, &c., 'by whom,' &c.	I. *da kiba*, 'by whom,' &c. (for all genders.)
Gen. *jong uba* (masc.), *jong kaba* (fem.), *jong iba* (dim.), 'whose,' &c.	G. *jong kiba*, 'whose.' (for all genders.)

Note.—On the (erroneous) use of the relative as a substitute for the emphatic, or Greek Definite Article. See remarks under § 200.

§ 52. *Compound Forms.*—How to render such words as 'whoever,' 'whichever,' 'whomsoever,' &c. in Khassi:—

1. *uno-uno-ruh-uba* (m.), whoever.
   ia uno-uno-ruh-uba, whomsoever.

   kano-kano-ruh-kaba (fem.), whoever.
   ia kano-kano-ruh-kaba, whomsoever.

   ino-ino-ruh-iba (dim.), whoever.
   ia-ino-ino-ruh-iba, whomsoever.

2. *uei-uei-ruh-uba* (m.), whoever, whatever.
   ka-ei-kaei-ruh-kaba (f.), whoever, whatever.

   iaei-iaei-ruh-ba (m.), whomsoever, whatever.
   ia uei-uei-ruh-uba (m.), whomsoever.
   ia kaei-kaei-ruh-kaba (f.), whomsoever.

   iei-iei-ruh-iba (dim.), whoever, whatever.
   ia-iei-iei-ruh-ba (dim.), whatever.

Other forms:

jaid-ba, (জাতি) whoever, whatever.
jár-ba, (যাঁহার) whoever, whatever.

Note 1.—Those which end in *-no* refer to persons; those in *-ei* may refer to persons, but chiefly to things.

Note. 2.—See under Indefinite Pronouns, § 55 *infra.*

Adjective Pronouns.

We shall explain the Adjective Pronouns under five classes, viz. Demonstrative, Distributive, Indefinite, Reflexive and Interrogative.

§ 53. The distinctive marks of the *Demonstrative Pronouns* are the suffixes *-ne, -ta, -to,-tai,* joined to each of the articles: 'this,' takes *-ne*; 'that' (in sight), takes *-to*; 'that' (very far, but dimly visible), takes *-tai*; 'that' (out of sight, or in contemplation), takes *-ta*.

(1) *-ne—une* (m.), *kane* (f.), *ine* (dim.), 'this;' *kine,* 'these.'

(2) *-to—uto* (m.), *kato* (f.), *ito* (dim.), 'that;' *kito* 'those.'

(3) *-ta—uta* (m.), *kata* (f.), *ita* (dim.), 'that;' *kita,* 'those.'

(4) *-tai—utai* (m.), *katai* (f.), *itai* (dim.), 'that;' *kitai,* 'those.'

No. 1. is close at hand, no. 2. is a little further, no. 3. is further still, and no. 4 is the furthest of all.

§ 54. *The Distributive Pronouns.*—The idea of distribution is expressed, (1) by the mere repetition of the pronoun; as,

uwei-uwei (m.), *kawei-kawei* (f.), *iwei-iwei* (dim.),	'each,' 'every,' 'one by one.'

(2) By prefixing *mar*, probably the Hindústaní هر (*har*) in هرايك (*har-ék*); see § 44, as,

mar-uwei, or *mar-uwei-uwei*, *mar-kawei*, or *mar-kawei-kawei*, *mar-iwei*, or *mar-iwei-iwei*,	'each,' 'one each.'

(3) By placing *-pa* between the pronouns repeated, thus—

wei-pa-wei (com.),
uwei-pa-uwei (m.),
kawei-pa-kawei (f.),
iwei-pa-iwei (dim.), } 'one by one,' 'each.'

uwei-pa-kawei (m. & f.), 'one by one,' (both male and female).

(4) Sometimes *ruh* also is added after the repetition:

uwei-uwei-ruh (m.), 'each one,' 'every one.'
kawei-kawei-ruh (f.), " " " "
iei-iei-ruh (dim.), " " " "

Uwei, kawei, often mean 'either,' and when followed by a negative mean 'neither.' See Syntax, § 195.

§ 55. *The Indefinite Pronouns.*—These are—

1. *baroh*, all.
2. *baroh-ár*, both.
3. *baroh-uwei* (m.), *baroh-kawei* (f.), *baroh-iwei* (dim.), } the whole.
4. *wei-pat* (com.) *uwei-pat* (m.), *kawei-pat* (fem.), *iwei-pat* (dim.), } another.
5. *uno-uno-ruh*, *kano-kano-ruh*, *ino-ino-ruh*, } any one.
6. *kino-kino-ruh*, some.
7. *kaei-kaei-ruh*, something.
8. *ei-ei-ruh*, something.
9. *bún, shibún*, many, much.

10. *khyndiat,* few.
11. *katto-katne,* some, more or less.
12. *uno-ruh-uno,* somebody or another.
13. *wei-ruh-wei,* somebody or another.
14. *kaei-ruh-kaei,* something or another.
15. *kano-ruh-kano,* someone (*fem.*), or another.
16. *ino-ruh-ino,* someone or another.
17. *iei-ruh-iei,* something or another.
18. *uno-uno-ruh-em,* no one, nobody (*m.*)
19. *kano-kano-ruh-ém,* no one, nobody (*fem.*)
20. *ino-ino-ruh-ém,* no one, nobody (*dim.*)
21. *kino-kino-ruh-ém,* done (*pl.*)
22. *kaei-kaei-ruh-ém,* nothing.
23. *ei-ei-ruh-ém,* nothing.
24. *shi-khad-dei,* much.
25. *khún-khyndiat,* very little.

§ 56. *Reflexive Pronouns.*—These always refer to the nominative of the verb, like the Bengali আপন (*ápan*) and the Hindustani اپنا, (*ápná*), and consist of *la,* 'his,' or some combinations of *la*; as, *la,* 'his;' *la ka jong,* 'my, thine, his, your, our, their or one's own;' *lade,* '(self), myself, thyself, himself, herself, themselves, yourself, yourselves, according to the number and person of the nominative:—

(1) Nga don *la* ka íng, 'I have *my* house.'
(2) U don *la* ka íng, 'He has *his* house.'
(3).U la pyllait *ia la de,* 'He liberated *himself.*'
(4) Nga don la ka jong ka íng, 'I have *my own* house.'
(5) U don la ka jong ka íng, 'He has *his own* house.'

See § 192 for a detailed explanation, and also of *hí*. The ordinary possessive particle *jong* would alone in the above examples refer the house to some person other than that represented by the nominative: thus—

Ka íng jong u= তাহার বাড়ী, اسکا گھر, his house.

La ka íng=আপন বাড়ী, اپنا گھر, his own house.

§ 57. *Interrogative Pronouns.—Ei?* who? (common gender)—*uei?* (m.), who?—*kaei?* (fem.), who?—*kiei?* (pl.), who?—*kano?* which?—*uno?* who?—*mano?* who? (com. gender), or who's there?—*ino?* (dim.), who? or which?—*iano?* for or to whom?—*hano?* to whom?—*jong no?* where? (com. gender)—*jong kaei?* of which?—*jong kano?* of which?—*jong kiei?* (pl.), whose?—*kino?* (pl.), who?—*aiuh?* what?—*nano?* from whom?—*badno?* with whom?

CHAPER VI.

Of the Verb.

§ 58. The verb asserts something of the subject; either what it does, or what it suffers; or, thirdly, that it exists in a certain state; as—

(1) U ksew u *wïar,* The dog barks.

(2) U khlá u *kyrhuh,* The tiger growls.

(3) *La pyniap* ia ka miáw, The cat was killed.

(4) *Yn sa khet* ia ka díng, The tree will be cut down.

(5) U Blei u *long*, God exists.

(6) U khynnah u *thïah*, The lad sleeps.

Note.—The conjugation of the verb is very simple, and what applies to one verb applies to all. Although no change whatever is effected in the radical form of the verb itself, still, by means of prepositions, pronouns, and other auxiliary particles of mood and tense, a regular system, answering to that of conjugation in the more elaborated class of languages, is formable. But before we come to this, other important facts touching the verb should be explained with more or less detail, ere the conjugation so called can be rendered intelligible, especially to foreign students of the dialect.

Classification of the Verbs.

§ 58. The Khassi verbs may be considered under two aspects—1st, in their relation to the other main parts of the sentence; 2ndly, as to their form.

The first principle of classification is applicable to all languages, and in this respect is the more comprehensive. The various terms used are *descriptive* of the relation in which the verb stands to other members of the sentence; thus, (1) when an action or state is considered as not *passing over* from the subject to an object, it is called an *Intransitive Verb*; as,

U ksár u *da phet*-noh, The fox is running away.
U myrsïang u *kynkáw*, The jackal yells.
Ka shnong ka *dang-pluh*, The village is still burning.

(2) When the verb expresses an action as *passing over*, from the subject to an object, it is called a *Transitive Verb;* as,

U ksár u *la rong-noh* ia ka sïar, The fox carried off the fowl.

Ka blang ka *bám* ia u kháw, The goat is eating the rice.

U bysein u *la puh* ia u khynnah, The snake bit the boy.

(3) When the verb expresses an action *indefinitely*, i. e., without reference to any particular subject, it is called an *Impersonal Verb;* thus,

Ki iathuh, They say = the French *on dit,* 'there is a rumour.'

Ka shit eh, It is very hot. *Ka la rang,* It is fine.

(4) When a particle is used to *assist* another verb by indicating either the *time* or the *manner* in which an action is performed, or in which any thing exists, it is called an *Auxiliary* of *Tense,* or an *Auxiliary* of *Mood;* as,

U *la* wan, He came.
U'*n* wan, He *will* come.
U'*n sa* wan, He *will* come *presently.*
U *dang* wan, He has *just* come.
U lah ba'n wan, He *can* come.
U'n *da* wan, He *would* come.
Lada u'n wan, *If* he comes.
U *dei* wan, He *ought* to come. He is due.

§ 59. The classification according to the *form,* which is

strictly etymological, is a key to one of the most prominent features of the Khassi language; thus,

(1) *Causative Verbs* take the prefix *pyn*, or, by assimilation, *pyl*, *pyr*, *pyd*. Causative verbs are of two classes, according as *pyn* is prefixed to a *transitive* or to an *intransitive* verb.

(*a*) Those formed from *intransitives* we shall call *causative* verbs of the *first* intention; as,

iaid, to walk; *pyn-iaid*, to drive, to put agoing.
jot, to perish; *pyn-jot*, to destroy.
duh, to vanish; *pyn-duh*, to annul.
háp, to fall; *pyn-háp*, to fell.
roi, to grow in size; *pyn-roi*, to augment.
mih, to rise; *pyn-mih*, to raise, to produce.
khih, to move; *pyn-khih*, to agitate.
shái, to shine; *pyn-shái*, to enlighten.
poi, to arrive; *pyn-poi*, to send.
long, to be; *pyn-long*, to create, to establish.
juh, to feel well at ease; *pyn-juh*, to tame, to subdue.
tíng, to be afraid; *pyn-tíng*, to frighten, to terrify.
ngeit, to believe; *pyn-ngeit*, to persuade.
íh, to see; *pyn-íh*, to show.
lait, to be at large; *pyl-lait*, to deliver, to set free.

(*b*) Causative verbs formed from *transitive* verbs, we would call causative verbs of the *second intention*, when the principal agent acts through an *intermediaire* or by proxy (this important distinction is often overlooked by foreigners); as,

bïa, to marry ; *pyn-bïa,* to give in marriage.
búd, to follow ; *pyn-búd,* to send after.
ong, to say ; *pyn-ong,* to deliver a message.
thuh, to know ; *pyr-thuh,* to imitate (another).
thied, to buy ; *pyn-thied,* to buy through another.
phah, to send ; *pyn-phah,* to send for, or through another.
len, to deny ; *pyn-len,* to deny through another.
kren, to speak ; *pyn-kren,* to speak for, or through another.

This is a very interesting feature of the language ; instead of saying "speak for me," a Khassi would say "cause me to speak through you :" *pyn-ong, pyn-kren,* and all this doing a thing 'by proxy,' is implied in *pyn.*

Note 1.—Causative verbs of the *first class,* change *intransitive* verbs into *transitive;* the *second* are a kind of *double transitives,* for they imply two agents, one acting *upon,* or *through,* or *for* another, as the case may be.

Note 2.—The prefix *pyn-* is most probably the same as the verb *pún,* 'to make,' 'to pave the way.'

(2) The second class according to the *form* are the *Frequentative Verbs,* which represent an action or state as repeated, continued, or persisted in. These take the prefix *iai-*, or the particles *dem, dup, nang, shait, ksáw :*

iai-leh, to do repeatedly ; *iai-iám,* to cry continually.
iai-duh, to have repeated losses ; *dem-wan,* to come often.
dem-kylli, to persist in asking ; *dem-pán,* to apply frequently.

dup-leh, to practise; *dup-nang*, to exercise.

nang-kylli, to ask again; *nang-wád*, to keep on searching.

shait-pang, to be always ill; *shait-kylli*, to be inquisitive, &c.

ksáw-bám (of the tiger, &c.), to be in the habit of devouring (men).

(3) *Inceptive Verbs*, which denote both the beginning of an action, and (often) a state of transition: *man* is the particle used; as,

man-sníw, to grow bad; *man-sàw*, to grow red.

man-'riwbhá, to grow rich; *man-stád*, to grow wise.

(4) *Reciprocal Verbs* embrace those by which the subject and object are represented as mutually both *cause* and *effect*, or equally participating in any action or state; the particle is *ia*.

ia-ïeit, to love one another; *ia-leh*, to quarrel, to fight.

ia-kajïa (কাজিয়া), to quarrel; *ia-kren*, to converse.

pïam, to embrace, *ia-pïam*, to embrace one another.

kop, to grasp, *ia-kop*, to raffle; *soh*, to stick, *ia-soh*, to unite.

nïa, to reason; *ia-nïa*, to dispute.

To this class we must consider a great number which imply consent, or willingness merely to belong, such as:

ia-leit, to go together; to go willingly.

ia-trei, to work together; *or* willingly.

ia-mih, to rise together; *or* with common consent.

The Turkish, also an important branch of the Turanian stock, has a similar particle *ich;* as, *sev-mek*, to love; *sevich-mek*, to love mutually.

(5) *Intensive Verbs* take the prefix *kyn, lyn, syn, tyn,* or by assimilation, *kyl-, kyr-, kym ; lym-, sym-,* &c., &c. Some of these verbs are scarcely distinguishable from the causative verbs in *pyn-*, and many of them have a *middle* or *subjective* force; as,

khró, to call, to lure; *synkhró,* to purr like a cat.
'rïah, a wicker basket; *synrïah,* meton. to sneeze (imitating water forced through a sieve).
kynjoh, to over-reach; *kynrïah,* to keep aloof.
syntúid, to slip, to slide; *kyníum,* to grumble.
kynsnok, to snore; *kyn-máw,* lit. to use a stone as a memorial, hence fig. to remember.
kynroh, to heap together, to make a wall (from *roh,* to accumulate); *kyntuh,* to incite, to spur on.
kynwin, to shake violently, to be agitated (from *win,* to be agitated); *kynúd,* to hum.
lympat, to smash; *sympat,* to thrash.
lynniár, to weep; *tynruh,* to poke.
lynshér, to thrust; *lynngoh,* to stare, to be astounded.
synshár, to rule; *kynruh,* to shake, to sift.

Remark 1.—Many of those in *kyn-* answer to Greek verbs in *-ίζω, -άζω ;* and to our English verbs in *-ize.*

Remark 2.—Nouns, adjectives and adverbs have also this prefix, showing the still very primitive stage; as, *kynran,* 'a coward' (also a verb); *tynjit,* 'stinking'; *tynáw,* 'antler, tusk'; *kyning,* 'still,' 'agape.'

THE MOODS AND TENSES.

We shall now explain with some detail the various particles of Mood and Tense, before giving the conjugation of Khassi Verbs.

§ 60. *Auxiliaries of Mood.*—These are *lah, nang, dei, da, ioh, tó, ià, ái* and *hó* (following the Verb).

(1) *Lah,* 'to be able,' is the sign of the Potential Mood; and, except in negative sentences, governs the verb in the Infinitive with *ba'n.* It denotes possibility, power or inclination:

U lah ba'n leit-noh, He can go away.

U'n ym lah ba'n iáid stet, He will not be able to walk fast; or, *U'n ym lah iaid stet eh,* He will not be able to walk very fast.

(2) *Nang,* besides denoting ability in general, expresses *mental* or *intellectual* ability, and should be used in preference to *lah* when the latter is meant, like জান in Bengali, and not পারন. *Permission* or *authority* to do a thing is expressed only by *lah,* but never by *nang;* as,

U nang thoh, He can write.

U nang trei, He can work.

U nang ba'n trei, He can work.

(3) *Ioh,* lit. 'to have,' like *lah,* often denotes *permission* or the *power* to do something; as,

Nga'n *ioh* leit, I will be able (or permitted) to go.

Nga'm *ioh* wan, I cannot come.

U'm put *ioh* trei, He is not yet able to work, He cannot (or, is not permitted to) work as yet.

(4) *Dei,* lit. 'it binds,' 'it is proper.' It is the Greek δεῖ in all its secondary meanings. As an auxiliary it is used impersonally with the Infinitive:

Ka dei ba'n konguh ia U Blei, We ought to obey God.

Ka dei ba'n sait la ka rám, We ought to clear our debts.

(5) *Da* adds uncertainty, or softens an expression:

U'n *da* wan, He *would* come.

Haba u *da* wan, *Should* he come.

U *da* kren shái, He *was* speaking out.

Haba u *da* leit, nga'n *da* sngowbha eh, *Should* he go, I *should* be much pleased.

§ 61. *Auxiliaries of Tense.*—These are *la, lah, yn, sa, nang, dang, da, wan.*

(1) *La* is the sign of the past tense, mostly of the *indefinite,* and sometimes of the *present complete.*

U briw u wan, The man comes.

U briw u *la* wan, The man has come.

(2) *La lah* is the sign of the *present perfect* (complete), and sometimes of the *past complete.*

U *la-lah* wan u briw, The man *has* come (pres. comp.)

U briw u *la lah* wan, mynba nga la poi, The man *had* come when I arrived (past complete).

(3) *Yn,* or after a vowel *'n,* is the sign of the *future:*

U briw u'*n* wan shisha, The man *will* surely come.

Yn wan shisha u briw, The man *will* come surely.

(4) *Sa* expresses the *immediate* future, either with or without *yn*:

U kypá u'*n* sa kren, His father will speak.

Without *yn* the natives use *sa*, chiefly in narration, or as a historical future:

Hadín kata u *sa* ái, Then he gave, lit. *will* give.

The natives always forget the true force of this particle when they translate or express their sentiments in English.

(5) *Nang* is also used as an auxiliary of tense, showing how principles now treated as essentially different, such as mood and tense, are at root derived the one from the other. As an auxiliary of tense, 1stly. it expresses a continued state or action:

U sím u *nang* iaid, The chief walks *on*.

U sím ruh u'n *nang* ia kren, The chief also will add some words.

2ndly. The subordinate idea of simultanëity with some other action or state is implied.

3rdly. Sometimes it expresses a state of progression:

U sím u nang pang, The chief is getting worse.

U soh u nang duna, The oranges are on the decrease.

Note.—To distinguish it from the mood auxiliary, *ba'n* should follow it before the Infinitive. See § 60 (2).

(6) *Dang*, lit. 'still,' 'just,' is the sign of the present incomplete, as well as of the simple present.

U dang iáp, He is just dead. (Present.)

U dang bám já, He is taking his food. (Incomplete.)

U dang pang, He is still unwell.

U dang lah bám, He has just taken his food.

(7) *Da* in many cases corresponds to our affix 'ing':

U briw u *da* trei minot eh, The man is working very hard.

(8) *Wan*, lit. 'to come,' is used in the complete tenses of the progressive form (§ 69, Indicative Mood), and similar to the use of *venir* in French:

U la wan tháw íng, He has been building a house.

U dang wan sum, He has just been bathing.

The Moods.

§ 62. The Moods express the manner in which an action takes place: 1. The verb may express an action or state in the form of an assertion. It is then said to be in the Indicative Mood; as,

U lúm u jerong eh, The mountain is very high.

U lúm u'm da jerong eh, The mountain is not very high.

2. An action or state may be expressed or supposed as possible, under certain conditions; the verb which expresses those conditions is said to be in the Subjunctive Mood; as,

Lada phi'm kren, nga'n kren, ma-nga hí, *If* you do not speak, I will speak myself.

Haba u da kren, nga'n ym ong ei-ei, *If* he should speak, I will not say a word.

L'ymda phi wan, ym don ba'n leit, *Unless* you come, no one will go there.

3. When the verb expresses either duty, obligation, power, permission, or ability, it is said to be in the Potential mood.

U snïang u'm nang khih, The pig cannot move.

Ka dei ia ngi ba'n trei, We ought to work.

Ka lah ba u'n kylla pat, He *may* change (his mind) again.

4. Verbs expressing commands in any form are said to be in the Imperative Mood; as, *leit,* 'go'; *thoh phi,* 'write' or 'you write'; *tó leit noh,* 'go away.' Form—Verb alone, or with *tó,* &c. before it; and *hó* after it.

1st pers. sing. requires *shah* (permit), or *ieh* (let), or *ái* (give, allow), followed by the future tense; as,

Tó shah nga'n wan sha phi! Let me come to you!

Tó ai nga'n wan ho! Let me come, will you?

1st pers. plur. requires *ià* and the future tense; as,

Ià, ngi'n ialeit-noh! Let us be off!

Ià, ngi'n ia trei-noh! Let us work away!

3rd pers. sing. and plur. require *ái, shah, tó ái,* with the future tense; as,

Ái u'n trei, Let him work.

Tó shah b'un trei, Let him work.

Tó phi'n shah bu'n wan mo! You'll let him come, won't you?

5. Actions or states expressed generally and indefinitely are in the Infinitive Mood; as,

Ba'n kren, 'to speak'; *iáp* or *ba'n iáp,* 'to die.'

Kaba kren, 'speaking'; *kaba iáp,* 'dying.'

The verb in its simple form without *ba'n* is an infinitive, *long*, 'to be'; *pang*, 'to be ill.' *Ba'n* implies, in a more or less emphatic way, design or purpose.

Note.—The supposed distinction between *ba'n* the sign of the infinitive and *ba* coupled with *yn* (will), in the form *ba'n* (in comparatives), is a pure invention; both are identical.

6. The English participle in 'ing' is easily distinguished in Khassi from the infinitive or verbal noun in 'ing,' by means of the particles *da, ia*. Thus:

He came *walking*, U la wan *da iaid.*
He came *running*, U la wan *ia-phet.*
He stood *smiling*, U la ïeng *ia-rykhíe.*

The Tenses.

§ 63. No change is effected in the radical form of any verb to express the various distinctions of time. The particles already explained under § 61 only are appropriated for that purpose.

(1) The Present Tense is expressed by the mere collocation of the verb with its nominative; as,

U pang, He is ill, *or* He ails.

(2) The Past by prefixing *la* or *la lah* to the simple verb; as,

U la pang, He was ill.
U la thoh, He wrote, *or* He has written.
U la wan, He came, *or* He has come.
also, U la *lah* wan, He *has* come.
U la *lah* thoh, He *has* written.

Note.—It is here we should explain that the form with *la* and *la lah* bears a different meaning when used in the principal clause of a compound or complex sentence:

Katba U la kren, nga la poi, As he spoke, I *arrived.*

Haba u la kren, nga la *lah* poi, When he spoke, I *had* arrived.

Mynba nga la poi, u la *lah* thoh, When I arrived, he *had* written.

In these examples, *la* is the past indefinite, and *la lah* the perfect complete. When used in a simple sentence both may be construed in the present complete, while *lah* or *la lah* would be emphatic :

U la wan u briw, The man has come.

U la *lah* wan u briw, The man *has* come.

This simple rule will help the foreign student considerably, and clear an apparent inconsistency in the use of these forms in the conjugation.

(3) The Future is expressed by prefixing *yn* (will), or *'n*, as a suffix to the article, *u'n, ka'n, i'n, ki'n,* 'He, she, it, they, will;' *yn sa* or *'n sa* for the approximate future, and *sa* for the future in narration:

U'n iám, He will weep.

U'n *sa* iám, He will weep (presently).

Ka'n iám, She will weep.

Ka'n *sa* iám, She will weep (presently).

Yn iam ki briw shibún haba u'n *sa* iap, Many people will weep when he dies (*pres. for immed. future*).

Ynda u la ioh sngow ia kata, u *sa* iám eh, After

he heard that, he *wept* bitterly (*past for future in narration*).

Note.—*Yn* is often used impersonally without the article:
Yn sa long, It will be (soon).

THE CONJUGATION OF THE VERB.

§ 64. *Long*, 'to be.'

Indicative Mood.

PRESENT.

Singular.	Plural.
1. *Nga long*, I am.	1. *Ngi long*, We are.
2. *Mé* or *Phá long*, Thou art.	2. *Phi long*, You are.
3. *U* or *Ka long*, He, she, *or* it is.	3. *Ki long*, They are.

PAST. See § 63, (2) *Note*.

Singular.	Plural.
1. *Nga la long*, I was.	1. *Ngi la long*, We were.
2. *Me* or *Phá la long*, Thou wast.	2. *Phi la long*, You were.
3. *U*, *Ka la long*, He, she, *or* it was.	3. *Ki la long*, They were.

FUTURE (*Indefinite*).

Singular.	Plural.
1. *Nga'n long*, I will be.	1. *Ngi'n long*, We will be.
2. *Me'n* or *Phá'n long*, Thou wilt be.	2. *Phi'n long*, You will be.
3. *U'n* or *Ka'n long*, He, she, *or* it will be.	3. *Ki'n long*, They will be.

(*Immediate Future.*)

1. *Nga'n sa long*, I am 2. *Me'n* or *Pha'n sa long*, Thou art 3. *U'n* or *Ka'n sa long*, He, *or* she is	about to be.	1. *Ngi'n sa long*, We are 2. *Phi'n sa long*, You are 3. *Ki'n sa long*, They are	about to be.

(*Future in Narration.*)

1. *Nga sa long.*	1. *Ngi sa long.*
2. *Me* or *Phá sa long.*	2. *Phi sa long.*
3. *U*, or *Ka sa long.*	3. *Ki sa long.*

Note.—This is always used in conjunction with some other state or action expressed in a dependent sentence in the *past* or *future*. For mode of rendering see Syntax.

PRESENT AND PAST COMPLETE.

Singular.		Plural.
1. *Nga la lah long*, I have or had 2. *Mé la lah long*, Thou hast or hadst 3. *U la lah long*, He has or had	been.	1. *Ngi la lah long*, We have or had been. 2. *Phi la lah long*, You have or had been. 3. *Ki la lah long*, They have or had been.

FUTURE COMPLETE.

Note.—Although it belongs more properly to the Syntax of the moods and tenses, we should here explain, that the form of the Future Perfect '*will have been*' depends on whether it comes in, in the PROTASIS, or *Dependent Clause,* or in the APODOSIS, or *Principal* clause of a compound sentence.

(*The Future Perfect or Complete in the Protasis.*)

1. *Haba nga'n da la lah long,* When I shall have been.
2. *Haba me'n da la lah long,* When thou wilt have been.
3. *Haba u'n da la lah long,* When he will have been.

PLURAL.

1. *Haba ngi'n da la lah long,* When we shall have been.
2. *Haba phi'n da la lah long,* When you will have been.
3. *Haba ki'n da la lah long,* When they will have been.

(*The future Complete in the Apodosis.*)

The simple form of the Present and Past Complete will suffice when the Protasis has the verb in the Future; thus :—

Haba phi'n poi, nga la lah kren.

When you WILL arrive, I SHALL HAVE SPOKEN.

Haba phi'n poi, u la lah kren.

When you WILL arrive, HE WILL HAVE SPOKEN.

Haba phi'n poi (Prot.), *nga la lah thoh* (Apodosis).

When you (WILL) arrive, I WILL HAVE WRITTEN.

Haba phi'n poi, u la lah thoh.

When you (WILL) arrive, HE WILL HAVE WRITTEN.

Note.—The past complete form *after* a dependent clause in the *Future Tense* has the force of the Future Perfect.

Subjunctive Mood.

PRESENT (*Supposition of a fact*).

1. *Lada nga long*, If I am.	1. *Lada ngi long*, If we are.
2. *Lada mé long*, If thou art.	2. *Lada phi long*, If you are.
3. *Lada u long*, If he is.	3. *Lada ki long*, If they are.

(*Supposition with Uncertainty*).

1. *Haba ngá da long*, If I be.	1. *Haba ngi da long*, If we be.
2. *Haba mé da long*, If thou be.	2. *Haba phi da long*, If you be.
3. *Haba u da long*, If he be.	3. *Haba ki da long*, If they be.

PAST INDEFINITE.

(*Unfulfilled Condition*).

1. *Lada nga la long*, If I was.	1. *Lada ngi la long*, If we were.
2. *Lada mé la long*, If thou wast.	2. *Lada phi la long*, If you were.
3. *Lada u la long*, If he was.	3. *Lada ki la long*, If they were.

(*Supposition with Uncertainty*).

1. *Haba nga da la long*, If I were.	1. *Haba ngi da la long*, If I were.
2. *Haba mé da la long*, If thou wert.	2. *Haba phi da la long*, If you were.
3. *Haba u da la long*, If he were.	3. *Haba ki da la long*, If they were.

Present and Past Complete.

(Supposition of a fact and Unfulfilled Condition.)

1. *Lada nga la lah long,* If I have or had	been.	1. *Lada ngi la lah long,* If we	have or had been.
2. *Lada mé la lah long,* If thou hast or hadst		2. *Lada phi la lah long,* If you	
3. *Lada u la lah long,* If he has or had		3. *Lada ki la lah long,* If they	

(Supposition with Uncertainty.)

1. *Haba nga da la lah long,* If I had been.	1. *Haba ngi da la lah long,* If we	had been.
2. *Haba mé da la lah long,* If thou hadst been.	2. *Haba phi da la lah long,* If you	
3. *Haba u da la lah long,* If he had been.	3. *Haba u da la lah long,* If they	

Simple Future.

(Supposition of a Fact.)

1. *Lada nga'n long,* If I shall be.	1. *Lada ngi'n long,* If we shall be.
2. *Lada mé'n long,* If thou wilt be.	2. *Lada phi'n long,* If you will be.
3. *Lada u'n long,* If he will be.	3. *Lada ki'n long,* If they will be.

(*Supposition with Uncertainty.*)

1. *Haba nga'n da long*, If I should be.
2. *Haba mé'n da long*, If thou shouldst be.
3. *Haba u'n da long*, If he should be.

1. *Haba ngi'n da long*, If we should be.
2. *Haba phi'n da long*, If you should be.
3. *Haba ki'n da long*, If they should be.

FUTURE COMPLETE.

(*Supposition of a Fact.*)

1. *Lada nga'n da la long*, If I shall have been.
2. *Lada mé'n da la long*, If thou shalt have been.
3. *Lada u'n da la long*, If he shall have been.

1. *Lada ngi'n da la long*, If we shall have been.
2. *Lada phi'n da lah long*, If you shall have been.
3. *Lada ki'n da la long*, If they shall have been.

(*Supposition with Uncertainty.*)

1. *Haba nga'n da la lah long*, If I should have been.
2. *Haba mé'n da la lah long*, If thou shouldst have been.
3. *Haba u'n da la lah long*, If he should have been.

1. *Haba ngi'n da la lah long*, If we should have been.
2. *Haba phi'n da la lah long*, If you should have been.
3. *Haba ki'n da la lah long*, If they should have been.

Note.—When the form *I should have been* expresses *obligation* or *duty*, it then refers to Past Time, and should be rendered by 'dei' with the infinitive. See § 60 (4), also POTENTIAL MOOD, p. 68.

Imperative Mood.

PRESENT.

1. *Tó ái nga'n long*, Let me be.
2. *Tó long*, or *Long ma-mé* (mas.), Be thou.
   Tó long ma-phá (fem.), Be thou.
3. *Tó ái u'n long*, Let him be.
   Tó ái ba u'n long, Let him be.
   Tó ái b'u'n long, Let him be.
   Tó ái ka'n long, Let her or it be.
   Tó ái ba ka'n long, Let her or it be.

1. *Tó ái ngi'n long*, Let us be.
   Tó ngi'n ia long, Let us be
2. *Tó long-phi*, Be ye.
   Tó ia long-phi, Be ye.
   Tó long-ma-phi, Be ye.
3. *Tó ái ki'n long*, Let them be.
   Tó ái ba ki'n long, Let them be.
   Tó ái yn long ma-ki, Let them be.
   Tó ái ba'n long ma-ki, Let them be.

Note 1.—Instead of 'ái' above, 'shah' (*to allow, to suffer*) may also be used, and is often used by the natives.

Note 2.—As commands, prayers, requests, &c., imply *futurity*, the Khassis form their Imperative with the future particle 'yn' or 'n (*will*).

Note 3.—'da' may precede 'long' in these examples.

Potential Mood.

Present and Future.

(*Possibility or Power.*)

Singular	Plural
1. *Nga lah ba'n long*, I may or can be.	1. *Ngi lah ba'n long* We
2. *Mé lah ba'n long*, Thou may'st or can'st be.	2. *Phi lah ba'n long*, You
3. *U lah ba'n long*, He may or can be.	3. *Ki lah ba'n long*, They

} may or can be.

(*Obligation or Duty*).

Singular	Plural
1. *Ka dei ia nga ba'n long*, I ought to be, or I should be.	1. *Ka dei ia ngi ba'n long*, We ought to be, or We should be.
2. *Ka dei ia mé ba'n long*, Thou oughtest to be, or Thou should'st be.	2. *Ka dei ia phi ba'n long*, You ought to be, or You should be.
3. *Ka dei ia u ba'n long*, He ought to be, or He should be.	3 *Ka dei ia ki ba'n long*, They ought to be, or They should be.

Past (*Possibility or Power.*)

Singular	Plural
1. *Ka lah, ba nga la long*, I might be.	1. *Ka lah, ba ngí la long* We might be.
2. *Ka lah, ba mé la long*, Thou mightest be.	2. *Ka lah, ba phi la long*, You might be.
3. *Ka lah, ba u la long*, He might be.	3. *Ka lah, ba ki la long*, They might be.

(*Obligation, Necessity or Duty.*)

1. *Ka la dei ia nga ba'n long,* I ought to have been.	1. *Ka la dei ia ngi ba'n long,* We ought to have been.
2. *Ka la dei ia mé ba'n long,* Thou should'st have been.	2. *Ka la dei ia phi ba'n long,* You should have been.
3. *Ka la dei ia u ba'n long,* He should have been.	3. *Ka la dei ia ki ba'n long,* They should have been.

FUTURE (*Possibility or Probability*), see PRESENT.

1. *Ka lah, ba nga'n long,* or *Lehse nga'n long,* I may be.
2. *Ka lah, ba mé'n long,* or *Lehse me'n long,* Thou may'st be.
3. *Ka lah, ba u'n long,* or *Lehse u'n long,* He may be.

PLURAL.

1. *Ka lah, ba ngi'n long,* or *Lehse ngi'n long,* We may be.
2. *Ka lah, ba phi'n long,* or *Lehse phi'n long,* You may be.
3. *Ka lah, ba ki'n long,* or *Lehse ki'n long,* They may be.

Note.—Ka lah, it is possible ; *Lehse,* perhaps.

(*Possibility with Uncertainty.*)

1. *Nga'n da lah ba'n long,* I could or might be.	1. *Ngi'n da lah ba'n long,* We could or might be.

2. *Me'n da lah ba'n long,* Thou could'st or might'st be.
3. *U'n da lah ba'n long,* He could or might be.

2. *Phi'n da lah ba'n long,* You could or might be.
3. *Ki'n da lah ba'n long,* They could or might be.

PRESENT COMPLETE.

(*Possibility and Probability.*)

1. *Ka lah, ba nga la lah long,* I may have been.
2. *Ka lah, ba mé la lah long,* Thou may'st have been.
3. *Ka lah, ba u la lah long,* He may have been.

PLURAL.

1. *Ka lah, ba ngi la lah long,* We may have been.
2. *Ka lah, ba phi la lah long,* You may have been.
3. *Ka lah, ba ki la lah long,* They may have been.

PAST COMPLETE.

1. *Nga'n da la lah ba'n long,* I might have been.
2. *Mé'n da la lah ba'n long,* Thou might'st have been.
3. *U'n da la lah ba'n long,* He might have been.

PLURAL.

1. *Ngi'n da la lah ba'n long,* We might have been.
2. *Phi'n da la lah ba'n long,* You might have been.
3. *Ki'n da la lah ba'n long,* They might have been.

Infinitive Mood.

PRESENT (*only*).

Long, or *Ba'n long,* to be.

Kaba long, being, to be (our Infinitive in '*ing*').

PAST (*is questionable*).

Ba'n la long, to have been. See § 226.

Participle.

ba long }
da long } being. See § 62, 6.
ia long }

ba la long, having been.

Note.—By substituting any other verb for 'long,' whether Transitive or Intransitive, the conjugation, according to the foregoing model, will universally apply; thus,

Thoh, to write; *Tháw*, to make; *Kren*, to speak.

PRESENT INDIC.—*Nga thoh*, I write.
Nga da thoh, I am writing.

PAST INDEF.—*Nga la thoh*, I wrote, or I have written.

FUTURE INDEF.—*Nga'n thoh*, I will write.
Nga'n sa thoh, I will write (soon).
Nga sa thoh (narrative, after a dependent clause in the Perfect tense).

PAST & PRES. COMPLETE.—*Nga la lah thoh*, I have or had written.

FUTURE COMPLETE.—*Nga'n da la lah thoh*, I will have written (after a conditional sentence).

PRESENT SUBJ.—*Lada nga thoh*, If I write.

Uncertainty { *Láda nga da thoh*, If I should write.
Haba nga da thoh, If I should write.

PAST SUBJ.—*Lada nga la thoh*, If I wrote.

PRES. & PAST COMP.—*Lada nga la lah thoh*, If I have or had written.

IMPERATIVE.—*To ái ba nga'n thoh*, Let me write.

POTENTIAL.—*Nga lah ba'n thoh*, I can write.

Obligation.—*Ka dei ia nga ba'n thoh,* I ought to write.

FUTURE.—*Ka lah ba nga'n thoh,* I may write.

Lehse nga'n thoh, I may write.

Possibility.—*Nga'n da lah ba'n thoh,* I might write.

Complete.—*Nga'n da la lah ba'n thoh,* I might have written.

The Negative Form.

§ 65. As the position and form of the negative particles in conjugating the verb is peculiar, and of great importance in Khassi, we give here an example of their use, that applies to all verbs used negatively. The principal particle of negation is *ym,* or after a vowel *'m,* 'not, no.' *Shym* is used in the past tense only to add emphasis to the usual particle *ym* or *'m,* as well as *put* (yet); thus,

Ym shym or *'m shym,* 'surely not, decidedly not,' that is, DID not, and *ym put* or *'m put,* 'not yet.'

When these forms are employed, besides a simple negation, an *emphatic contradiction* is also implied, *U la wan mo? E'm, u'm shym wan,* "He came, did he not?" "No! he did *not* come."—*U la úr u briw? E'm u'm shym úr.* "Did the man fall?" "No! he did *not* fall."

Indicative Mood.

PRESENT.

1. *Nga'm da thoh,* *Nga'm thoh,*	I do not write.	1. *Ngi'm da thoh,* *Ngi'm thoh,*	We do not write.
2. *Mé'm da thoh,* *Mé'm thoh,*	Thou dost not write.	2. *Phi'm da thoh,* *Phi'm thoh,*	You do not write.

3. *U'm da thoh,* *U'm thoh,* } He does not write.	3. *Ki'm da thoh,* *Ki'm thoh,* } They do not write.

PAST.

1. *Nga'm shym thoh,* I did not write.	1. *Ngi'm shym thoh,* We did not write.
2. *Mé'm shym thoh,* Thou didst not write.	2. *Phi'm shym thoh,* You did not write.
3. *U'm shym thoh,* He did not write.	3. *Ki'm shym thoh,* They did not write.

FUTURE.

1. *Nga'n ym thoh,* I will not write.	1. *Ngi'n ym thoh,* We will not write.
2. *Mé'n ym thoh,* Thou wilt not write.	2. *Phi'n ym thoh,* You will not write.
3. *U'n ym thoh,* He will not write.	3. *Ki'n ym thoh,* They will not write.

PRESENT COMPLETE.

1. *Nga'm shym la thoh,* I have	not written.	1. *Ngi'm shym la thoh,* We have	not written.
2. *Mé'm shym la thoh,* Thou hast		2. *Phi'm shym la thoh,* You have	
3. *U'm shym la thoh,* He has		3. *Ki'm shym la thoh,* They have	

PAST COMPLETE.

1. *Nga'm shym la lah thoh,* I had not written.	1. *Ngi'm shym la lah thoh,* We had not written.

2. *Mé'm shym la lah thoh,* Thou hadst not written.

3. *U'm shym la lah thoh,* He had not written.

2. *Phi'm shym la lah thoh,* You had not written.

3. *Ki'm shym la lah thoh,* They had not written.

Subjunctive Mood.

PRESENT.

1. *Lada nga'm thoh,* If I do not write.
2. *Lada me'm thoh,* If thou dost not write.
3. *Lada u'm thoh,* If he does not write.

1. *Lada ngi'm thoh,* If we do not write.
2. *Lada phi'm thoh,* If you do not write.
3. *Lada ki'm thoh,* If they do not write.

(*Uncertainty.*)

1. *Haba nga'm da thoh,* If I do not write.
2. *Haba mé'm da thoh,* If thou do not write.
3. *Haba u'm da thoh,* If he do not write.

1. *Haba ngi'm da thoh,* If we do not write.
2. *Haba phi'm da thoh,* If you do not write.
3. *Haba ki'm da thoh,* If they do not write.

PAST.

1. *Lada nga'm shym thoh,* If I did not write.
2. *Lada mé'm shym thoh,* If thou didst not write.
3. *Lada u'm shym thoh,* If he did not write.

1. *Lada ngi'm shym thoh,* If we did not write.
2. *Lada phi'm shym thoh,* If you did not write.
3. *Lada ki'm shym thoh,* If they did not write.

FUTURE.

1. *Lada nga'n ym thoh,* If I shall not write.
2. *Lada me'n ym thoh,* If thou wilt not write.
3. *Lada u'n ym thoh,* If he will not write.

1. *Lada ngi'm ym thoh,* If we will not write.
2. *Lada phi'n ym thoh,* If you will not write.
3. *Lada ki'n ym thoh,* If they will not write.

(*Uncertainty.*)

1. *Haba nga'n ym da thoh,* If I were not to write.
2. *Haba me'n ym da thoh,* If thou wert not to write.
3. *Haba u'n ym da thoh,* If he were not to write.

1. *Haba ngi'n ym da thoh,* If we were not to write.
2. *Haba phi'n ym da thoh,* If you were not to write.
3. *Haba ki'n ym da thoh,* If they were not to write.

PRESENT COMPLETE.—*Lada nga'm shym la thoh, &c.,* If I have not written.

(*Uncertainty*)—*Haba nga'm shym da la thoh, &c.,* If I have not written.

PAST COMPLETE.—*Lada nga'm shym la lah thoh, &c.,* If I had not written.

(*Uncertainty*).—*Haba nga'm shym da la lah thoh,* If I had not written.

Potential Mood.

PRESENT—*MAY, CAN,* &c.

(*Power denied.*)

1. *Nga'm lah thoh,* I may or can not write.

1. *Ngi'm lah thoh,* We may or can not write.

2. *Mé'm lah thoh,* Thou mayest, &c., not write.
3. *U'm lah thoh,* He may or can not write.

2. *Phi'm lah thoh,* You may, &c., not write.
3. *Ki'm lah thoh,* They may, or can not write.

MAY.

(*Supposed denial.*)

1. *Ka lah ba nga'm thoh,* I may not write.
2. *Ka lah ba mé'm thoh,* Thou may'st not write.
3. *Ka lah ba u'm thoh,* He may not write.

1. *Ka lah ba ngi'm thoh,* We may not write.
2. *Ka lah ba phi'm thoh,* You may not write.
3. *Ka lah ba ki'm thoh,* They may not write.

Or,

1. *Leh' nga'm thoh,* I may not write.
2. *Leh' mé'm thoh,* Thou may'st not write.
3. *Leh' u'm thoh,* He may not write.

1. *Leh' ngi'm thoh,* We may not write.
2. *Leh' phi'm thoh,* You may not write.
3. *Leh, ki'm thoh,* They may not write.

Note.—Leh', contr. of *lehse,* perhaps. See *Note,* p. 69.

MUST, OUGHT, SHOULD (*Obligation.*)

1. *Ka'm dei ia nga ba'n thoh,* I ought or should not write.
2. *Ka'm dei ia mé ba'n thoh,* Thou oughtest or shouldst not write.

1. *Ka'm dei ia ngi ba'n thoh,* We ought or should not write.
2. *Ka'm dei ia phi ba'n thoh,* You ought, or should not write.

3. *Ka'm dei ia u ba'n thoh*, He ought or should not write.

3. *Ka'm dei ia ki ba'n thoh*, They ought or should not write.

WOULD (*Volition denied.*)

1. *Nga'n ym da thoh*, I would not write.
2. *Mé'n ym da thoh*, Thou would'st not write.
3. *U'n ym da thoh*, He would not write.

1. *Ngi'n ym da thoh*, We would not write.
2. *Phi'n ym da thoh*, You would not write.
3. *Ki'n ym da thoh*, They would not write.

PRESENT COMPLETE.

1. *Ka lah ba nga'm shym thoh*, I may have not written.
2. *Ka lah ba mé'm shym thoh*, Thou may'st have not written.
3. *Ka lah ba u'm shym thoh*, He may have not written.

1. *Ka lah ba ngi'm shym thoh*, We may have not written.
2. *Ka lah ba phi'm shym thoh*, You may have not written.
3. *Ka lah ba ki'm shym thoh*, They may have not written.

Or,

1. *Ka lah ba nga'm shym la thoh.*
2. *Ka lah ba mé'm shym la thoh.*
3. *Ka lah ba u'm shym la thoh.*

1. *Ka lah ba ngi'm shym la thoh.*
2. *Ka lah ba phi'm shym la thoh.*
3. *Ka lah ba ki'm shym la thoh.*

Or,

1. *Leh', nga'm shym la thoh.*	1. *Leh' ngi'm shym la thoh.*
2. *Leh', mé'm shym la thoh.*	2. *Leh' phi'm shym la thoh.*
3. *Leh' u'm shym la thoh.*	3. *Leh, ki'm shym la thoh.*

Lit.—Perhaps I have not written; I may have not written.

PAST INDEFINITE.

COULD, MIGHT (*Power denied.*)

1. *Nga'm shym lah ba'n thoh,* I could or might not write.	1. *Ngi'm shym lah ba'n thoh,* We could or might not write.
2. *Mé'm shym lah ba'n thoh,* Thou could'st or mightest not write.	2. *Phi'm shym lah ba'n thoh,* You could or might not write.
3. *U'm shym lah ba'n thoh,* He could or might not write.	3. *Ki'm shym lah ba'n thoh,* They could or might not write.

Note.—The form "*Nga'm la lah ba'n thoh*"
"*Mé'm la lah ba'n thoh*"
would seem technically correct, but is seldom used by the natives in *assertions*; though it is used in interrogatives, thus,

Nga'm la lah ba'n thoh? Was I not able to write?

PAST INDEFINITE. (*Supposed negation.*)

1. *Ka lah, ba nga'm shym thoh,* I might not write.	1. *Ka lah, ba ngi'm shym thoh,* We might not write.
2. *Ka lah, ba mé'm shym*	2. *Ka lah, ba phi'm shym*

thoh, Thou mightest not write.

3. *Ka lah, ba u'm shym thoh,* He might not write.

thoh, You might not write.

3. *Ka lah, ba ki'm shym thoh,* They might not write.

Note.—All this form is like that for the PRESENT COMPLETE, which in English also is closely allied in meaning to this PAST INDEFINITE. *I might write* sometimes conveys the same meaning as *I may have written.*

PAST COMPLETE.

COULD (*Power denied.*)

1. *Nga'n ym da la lah ba'n thoh,* I could not have written.
2. *Mé'n ym da la lah ba'n thoh,* Thou could'st not have written.
3. *U'n ym da la lah ba'n thoh,* He could not have written.

PLURAL.

1. *Ngi'n ym da la lah ba'n thoh,* We could not have written.
2. *Phi'n ym da la lah ba'n thoh,* You could not have written.
3. *Ki'n ym da la lah ba'n thoh,* They could not have written.

(*Power asserted negatively.*)

1. *Nga'n da la lah ba'n ym thoh,* I could have not written.
2. *Mé'n da la lah ba'n ym thoh,* Thou could'st have not written.

3. *U'n da la lah ba'n ym thoh,* He could have not written, or I might have not written, Thou mightest have not written, &c.

PLURAL.

1. *Ngi'n da la lah ba'n ym thoh,* We could have not written.
2. *Phi'n da la lah ba'n ym thoh,* You could have not written.
3. *Ki'n da la lah ba'n ym thoh,* They could have not written, or We might have not written, You might have not written, &c.

(*Doubt asserted negatively.*)

SINGULAR.

1. *Ka lah, ba nga'm shym la lah thoh,* I might not have written.
2. *Ka lah, ba mé'm shym la lah thoh,* Thou mightest not have written.
3. *Ka lah, ba u'm shym la lah thoh,* He might not have written.

PLURAL.

1. *Ka lah, ba ngi'm shym la lah thoh,* We may not have written.
2. *Ka lah, ba phi'm shym la lah thoh,* You might not have written.
3. *Ka lah, ba ki'm shym la lah thoh,* They may not have written.

Lit.—It is possible that we, &c., had not written.

Note.—How the position of the negative *ym* changes

in the above forms, *could,* or *might not have written,* and *could,* or *might have not written.*

Or,

1. *Leh' nga'm shym la lah thoh,* lit. Perhaps I had not written.
2. *Leh' mé'm shym la lah thoh,* lit. Perhaps Thou had'st not written.
3. *Leh' u'm shym la lah thoh,* lit. Perhaps he had not written.

PLURAL.

1. *Leh' ngi'm shym la lah thoh,* lit. Perhaps we had not written.
2. *Leh' phi'm shym la lah thoh,* lit. Perhaps you had not written.
3. *Leh' ki'm shym la lah thoh,* lit. Perhaps they had not written.

i.e., I, you, they, &c., might not have written.

Note.—This form applies to Principal Clauses in Complex Sentences.

OUGHT, MUST, SHOULD.

(*Obligation.*)

SINGULAR.

1. *Ka'm shym la dei ia nga ba'n thoh,* I ought not to have written, or should not have written.
2. *Ka'm shym la dei ia mé ba'n thoh,* Thou oughtest not to have written.
3. *Ka'm shym la dei ia u ba'n thoh,* He ought not to have written, or should not have written.

PLURAL.

1. *Ka'm shym la dei ia ngi ba'n thoh,* We ought not to have written, or should not have written.
2. *Ka'm shym la dei ia phi ba'n thoh,* You ought not to have written, or should not have written.
3. *Ka'm shym la dei ia ki ba'n thoh,* They ought not to have written, or should not have written.

WOULD.

(*Inclination.*)

1. *Nga'n ym da la lah thoh,* I would not have written.	1 *Ngi'n ym da la lah thoh,* We would not have written.
2. *Mé'n ym da la lah thoh,* Thou would'st not have written.	2. *Phi'n ym da la lah thoh,* You would not have written.
3 *U'm ym da la lah thoh,* He would not have written.	3. *Ki'n ym da la lah thoh,* They would not have written.

Note.—Mark the difference between *lah* here as an auxiliary of TENSE and *lah* as an auxiliary of mood followed by the Infinitive (*ba'n*) as above, 'could.' See §§ 60, 61, and under "Potential," page 93.

FUTURE (*Power denied*).

1. *Nga'n ym da lah ba'n thoh,* I could not write.	1. *Ngi'n ym da lah b'an thoh,* We could not write.
2. *Me'n ym da lah ba'n*	2. *Phi'n ym da lah ba'n*

thoh, Thou could'st not write.

3. *U'n ym da lah ba'n thoh,* He could not write.

thoh, You could no write.

3. *Ki'n ym da lah ba'n thoh,* They could not write.

Note.—See again another form bearing the same translation, but with a reference to the *past,* under PAST INDEFINITE above, page 78.

MIGHT.

(*Possibility asserted negatively.*)

1. *Ka lah ba nga'n ym da thoh,* I might not write.
2. *Ka lah ba me'n ym da thoh,* Thou mightest not write.
3. *Ka lah ba u'n ym da thoh,* He might not write.

1. *Ka lah ba ngi'n ym da thoh,* We might not write.
2. *Ka lah, ba phi'n ym da thoh,* You might not write.
3. *Ka lah, ba ki'n ym da thoh,* They might not write.

Note.—This form *without* "ḍa" would be correct, and applicable also under "MAY," p. 76.

OUGHT, SHOULD, MUST.

(*Obligation, duty, &c.*)

1. *Ka'n ym dei ia nga ba'n thoh,* I ought, should, &c., not write.
2. *Ka'n ym dei ia mé ba'n thoh,* Thou should'st, &c., not write.
3. *Ka'n ym dei ia u ba'n thoh,* He should not write.

PLURAL.

1. *Ka'n ym dei ia ngi ba'n thoh,* We should, &c., not write.
2. *Ka'n ym dei ia phi ba'n thoh,* You should, &c., not write.
3. *Ka'n ym dei ia ki ban thoh,* They should, &c., not write.

Note.—Another form bearing same translation, but with a reference to the *present* under PRESENT above, p. 76.

EXAMPLES (*Conditional sentences*).

1. *Lada nga la lah tip ia kata, nga'n ym da la lah thoh,* If I had known that, I would not have written.
2. *Lada nga la lah tip ia kata, Nga'n da la lah ba'n ym thoh,* If I had known that, I might have not written. Mark the position of *ym.* *Note,* p. 80.

(*Assertion.*)

3. *U la ong, ba ka lah ba u'm shym la lah kren ia kata,* He said, that he might have spoken that.
4. *U la ong, lehse u'm shym la lah iathuh ia kata,* He said, he might not have said that.
5. *Lada nga la ioh ih ia u hi, leh' nga'n ym da la lah ong ei-ei,* If I had seen him himself, I might not have said anything.
6. *Haba u da leit, Nga'n ym da shong Hangne,* If he went, I would not stay here.

Imperative.

1. *Wat ái ba nga'n thoh,* Do not let me write.	1. *Wat ái ba ngi'n thoh,* Do not let us write.
2. *Wat thoh, mé!* Do not write, thou!	2. *Wat thoh, phi,* Do not write, will you.
3. *Wat ái b'u'n thoh,* Do not let them write.	3. *Wat ái ba ki'n thoh,* Do not let them write.

Or (for 1st and 3rd pers. sing. and plural),

1. *Tó ái ba ngi'n ym thoh,* Let us not write.
2 *Tó ái ba ki'n ym thoh,* Let them not write.

Lit.—Do allow, that we, they, shall not write.

Or,

1. *Wat ái ia nga ba'n thoh,* lit., Do not allow me to write.
2. *Wat ái ia u ba'n thoh,* lit., Do not allow him to write.
3. *Wat ái ia ngi ba'n thoh,* lit., Do not allow us to write.
4. *Wat ái ia ki ba'n thoh,* lit., Do not allow them to write.

Note.—The Khassi negative particle of command *wat* is evidently the same as مت (*mat*) in Hindustani, *do not.*

Infinitive.

PRESENT.

Ba'n ym thoh, Not to write.
Ba'n ym da thoh, Not to be writing.
Ka b'ym thoh, Not writing.

PAST.

Ba'n ym la thoh, Not to have written.

Participle.

PRESENT.—*B'ym thoh,* i.e., *ba ym thoh,* Not writing.
PAST.—*B'ym la thoh,* Not having written.

POSITION OF PÙT, 'YET.'

§ 66. *Pùt* is never used, except in negative propositions, like *shym*, and it is important to point out its position in a sentence; which is always immediately after the negative particle *ym* or *'m.*

EXAMPLES.

Nga'm thoh, I do not write.
Nga'm put thoh, I have not yet written.
Nga'm put shym thoh, I have not yet written.
Nga'm put shym la thoh, I have not yet written.
Nga'm put shym la lah thoh, I had not yet written.
Nga'n ym put thoh, I will not write (as) yet.

THE PASSIVE VOICE.

§ 67. Strictly speaking, the Khassi language, like the dialects of the adjacent mountain tribes, has no Passive Voice. The so-called *Passive,* is formed by omitting the subject; and so, using the verb indefinitely or impersonally with the object following the verb in the accusative with *ia.* Let us take the verb *ïeit,* 'to love.'

Present.

1. *Dang ïeit ia nga,* I am loved.	1. *Dang ïeit ia ngi,* We are loved.
2. *Dang ïeit ia mé,* Thou art loved.	2. *Dang ïeit ia phi,* You are loved.
3. *Dang ïeit ia u,* He is loved.	3. *Dang ïeit ia ki,* They are loved.

This may also be translated, "I am still loved."

Past.

1. *La ïeit ia nga,* I was loved.	1. *La ïeit ia ngi,* We were loved.
2. *La ïeit ia mé,* Thou wast loved.	2. *La ïeit ia phi,* You were loved.
3. *La ïeit ia u,* He was loved.	3. *La ïeit ia ki,* They were loved.

Future Indefinite.

1. *Yn ïeit ia nga,* I shall be loved.	1. *Yn ïeit ia ngi,* We shall be loved.
2. *Yn ïeit ia mé,* Thou shalt or wilt be loved.	2. *Yn ïeit ia phi,* You will be loved.
3. *Yn ïeit ia u,* He shall or will be loved.	3. *Yn ïeit ia ki,* They will be loved.

Immediate Future.

1. Y*n sa ïeit ia nga,* I shall be loved.	1. *Yn sa ïeit ia ngi,* We shall be loved.

2. *Yn sa ïeit ia mé,* Thou wilt be loved.
3. *Yn sa ïeit ia u,* He will be loved.

2. *Yn sa ïeit ia phi,* You will be loved.
3. *Yn sa ïeit ia ki,* They will be loved.

Present Complete.

1. *La dang ïeit ia nga,* I have been loved.
2. *La dang ïeit ia mé,* Thou hast been loved.
3. *La dang ïeit ia u,* He has been loved.

1. *La dang ïeit ia ngi,* We have been loved.
2. *La dang ïeit ia phi,* You have been loved.
3. *La dang ïeit ia ki,* They have been loved.

Past Complete.

1. *La lah ïeit ia nga,* I had been loved.
2. *La lah ïeit ia mé,* Thou hadst been loved.
3. *La lah ïeit ia u,* He had been loved.

1. *La lah ïeit ia ngi,* We had been loved.
2. *La lah ïeit ia phi,* You had been loved.
3. *La lah ïeit ia ki,* They had been loved.

This form may be used also for the *Present Complete.*

Or,

1. *La jiw ïeit ia nga.*
2. *La jiw ïeit ia mé.*
3. *La jiw ïeit ia u.*

1. *La jiw ïeit ia ngi.*
2. *La jiw ïeit ia phi.*
3. *La jiw ïeit ia ki.*

Lit.—I used to be loved. We used to be loved, &c. That is : I have been loved, or, I had been loved, according to the context or accompanying circumstances. *Jiw* = "used to."

Subjunctive Mood.

PRESENT.

(Supposition of a fact.)

1. *Lada ïeit ia nga,* If I am loved.	1. *Lada ïeit ia ngi,* If we are loved.
2. *Lada ïeit ia mé,* If thou art loved.	2. *Lada ïeit ia phi,* If you are loved.
3. *Lada ïeit ia u,* If he is loved.	3. *Lada ïeit ia ki,* If they are loved.

INCOMPLETE.

Lada dang ïeit ia nga, ia mé, ia u, If I am, &c., being loved.	*Lada dang ïeit ia ngi, ia phi, ia ki,* If we, you, they, are being loved.

(Supposition with uncertainty.)

1. *Haba da ïeit ia nga,* If I be loved.	1. *Haba da ïeit ia ngi,* If we be loved.
2. *Haba da ïeit ia nga,* If thou be loved.	2. *Haba da ïeit ia phi,* If you be loved.
3. *Haba da ïeit ia u,* If he be loved.	3. *Haba da ïeit ia ki,* If they be loved.

PAST.

1. *Lada la ïeit ia nga,* If I were loved.	1. *Lada la ïeit ia ngi,* If we were loved
2. *Lada la ïeit ia mé,* If thou wert loved.	2. *Lada la ïeit ia phi,* If you were loved.
3. *Lada la ïeit ia u,* If he were loved.	3. *Lada la ïeit ia ki,* If they were loved.

Present and Past Complete.

1. *Lada la lah ïeit ia nga*, If I have been loved.	1. *Lada la lah ïeit ia ngi*, If we have been loved.
2. *Lada la lah ïeit ia mé*, If thou hast been loved.	2. *Lada la lah ïeit ia phi*, If you have been loved.
3. *Lada la lah ïeit ia u*, If he has been loved.	3. *Lada la lah ïeit ia ki*, If they have been loved.

Or,

It may be rendered, If I, we, you, &c., had been loved.

Future.

(*Supposition of a fact.*)

1. *Lada yn ïeit ia nga*, If I shall be loved.	1. *Lada yn ïeit ia ngi*, If we will be loved.
2. *Lada yn ïeit ia mé*, If thou wilt be loved.	2. *Lada yn ïeit ia phi*, If you will be loved.
3. *Lada yn ïeit ia u*, If he will be loved.	3. *Lada yn ïeit ia ki*, If they will be loved.

(*Supposition of uncertainty.*)

1. *Haba'n da ïeit ia nga*, If I should be loved.	1. *Haba'n da ïeit ia ngi*, If we should be loved.
2. *Haba'n da ïeit ia mé*, If thou should be loved.	2. *Haba'n da ïeit ia phi*, If you should be loved.
3. *Haba'n da ïeit ia u*, If he should be loved.	3. *Haba'n da ïeit ia ki*, If they should be loved.

FUTURE COMPLETE.

1. *Haba'n da la ïeit ia nga.*	1. *Haba'n da la ïeit ia ngi.*
2. *Haba'n da la ïeit ia mé.*	2. *Haba'n da la ïeit ia phi.*
3. *Haba'n da la ïeit ia u.*	3. *Haba'n da la ïeit ia ki.*

If I, thou, he, we, &c., should have been loved.

Potential Mood.

For all the Passive Forms in this Mood the Khassis use the *Active Voice.* For example :—

(1) If he had done so, he would have been loved by all.
Lada u la lah leh kumta, u'n da la long, BA LA ÏEIT (loved) *da ki briw baroh ;* or,
Lada u la lah leh kumta, baroh ki'n DA LA LAH ÏEIT *ia u.*

(2) He should have been loved by all, *Ka la dei ba ki'n da ïeit ia u baroh.*

Imperative.

The same remark is also applicable to this Mood; a *Passive Form* is unusual, if ever used; though it would not be difficult to form one. The following would be correct :—

To shah, ba yn ïeit ia nga.
To ái, ba yn ïeit ia nga. } Let me be loved.

But *shah* and *ái* (allow, permit) generally require a personal rather than an impersonal Verb after them, as—

To shah ba ki'n ïeit ia nga.
To ái ba ki'n ïeit ia nga. } Let them love me.

Infinitive.

PRESENT.—*Ba yn ïeit* or *ba'n long ba la ïeit,* To be loved.

PRESENT PERFECT OR COMPLETE.—This is expressed by the Present (*Active*), with the governing Verb in the *Past Complete :—*

(*Active*).—*Ka la lah dei ia u ba'n ïeit,* He ought TO HAVE LOVED.

(*Passive*).—*Ka la lah dei ba'n ïeit ia u,* He ought TO HAVE BEEN LOVED.

Note.—Obligation as implied in the English Infinitive Passive, is expressed in Khassi (as in French *fallu*) by the governing Verb " dei."

Participle.

PAST.—*Ba la ïeit,* Loved.

PRESENT COMPLETE.—*Ba la lah ïeit,* Having been loved.

Of the use of the

NEGATIVE IN THE PASSIVE.

§ 68. For reasons similar to those stated under § 65, we here give the order to be observed in the formation of negative sentences in the Passive Voice. The negative *ym* (not), or the emphatic *ym shym, ym put,* or *'m, 'm shym, 'm put,* must always *follow* the auxiliary *yn* or *'n,* and *precede* the principal verb and its other auxiliaries *lah, la, dang,* &c.

Indicative.

PRESENT.—*Ym ïeit ia nga,* I am not loved.

FUTURE.—*Yn ym ïeit ia nga,* I shall not be loved.

PAST.—*Ym shym ïeit ia nga,* I was not loved.

PRESENT COMPLETE.—*Ym shym la ïeit ia nga,* I have not been loved.

PAST COMPLETE.—*Ym shym la lah ïeit ia nga,* I had not been loved.

Subjunctive.

PRESENT.—*Lada ym ïeit ia nga,* If I am not loved.
Haba ym da ïeit ia nga, uncertainty), If I be not loved.

FUTURE.—*Lada yn ym ïeit ia nga,* If I shall not be loved.
Haba yn ym da ïeit ia nga, (uncertainty), If I should not be loved.

PAST.—*Lada ym shym ïeit ia nga,* If I were not loved.

PAST COMPLETE.—*Lada ym shym la lah ïeit ia nga,* If I had not been loved.

Potential.

PRESENT.—*Ym lah ïeit ia nga,* I cannot be loved.

FUTURE.—*Yn ym lah ïeit ia nga,* I could not be loved.

PAST.—*Ym shym da lah ba'n ïeit ia nga.* } I could not
Ym jiw lah ba'n ïeit ia nga. } be loved.

OUGHT, MUST, SHOULD NOT (*Obligation, Necessity*).
Ym dei ba'n ïeit ia nga, I should not be loved.

Ym shym la dei ba'n ïeit ia nga, I should not have been loved.

MAY (*Probability*).

Lehse yn ym ïeit ia nga, I may not be loved; *Or,*
Leh' yn ym ïeit ia nga, I may not be loved.
Lit.—Perhaps I will not be loved.

Imperative.

PRESENT.

1. *Tó ái ba yn ym ïeit ia nga,* Let me not be loved.
2. *Tó ái ba yn ym ïeit ia mé,* Be thou not loved.
3. *Tó ái ba yn ym ïeit ia u,* Let him not be loved.

PLURAL.

1. *Tó ái ba yn ym ïeit ia ngi,* Let us not be loved.
2. *Tó ái ba yn ym ïeit ia phi,* Be ye not loved.
3. *Tó ái ba yn ym ïeit ia ki,* Let them be loved.

Note.—The above form, though correct and according to analogy, is still unusual; the Khassis prefer the active or personal construction. Thus in the *Indicative* they would say :—

U'm ai ba'n ïeit ia nga, He does not allow (them) to love me.

U'm shah ba'n ïeit ia nga, He does not suffer (them) to love me.

U'm mon ba'n shoh ia nga, He is not willing or does not like (them) to strike me.

So also in the *Imperative Mood* they would use a personal form, thus :—

Wat ai ba ki'n ïeit ia nga, Do not let them love me.
Lit.—Do not permit, that they will love me.
= Let me not be loved.

Or,

1. *Wat ái ba yn ïeit ia nga,* Do not let me be loved.
2. *Wat ái ba yn ïeit ia mé,* Be thou not loved.
3. *Wat ái ba yn ïeit ia u,* Do not let him be loved.

Infinitive.

PRESENT.—*Ba'n ym long ba la ïeit,* Not to be loved. This is distinguishable only from the whole context, and generally requires in Khassi to be followed by the agent with *da,* as *ba la ïeit* may have an *active* sense.

Ba'n ym long ba la ïeit DA KI BRIW, *kaba sngowsih eh,* Not to be loved (*by people*) is very deplorable.

PAST.—*Ba'n ym long ba la lah ïeit,* Not to have been loved.

Participle.

PRESENT.—*B'ym ïeit,* Not loved.
PAST.—*B'ym la ïeit,* Not been loved.
COMPLETE.—*B'ym shym la ïeit,* Not having been loved.

PROGRESSIVE FORM.

§ 69. Under § 59, 2, we have referred to an important class of verbs formed by the constant use of the prefix *iai,* and the particles *dang, nang,* and others. Many of these are employed by the natives to express an *action* or *state* as *progressive* or incomplete, and perform so prominent a part, that they call for special attention, although direct and long intercourse with the natives only could enable the foreigner to comprehend fully, and correctly apply the construction. We shall here take the verb *tháw*, 'to make or build,' for our model.

Active Voice.

INDICATIVE MOOD.

PRESENT.—*U dang-tháw (íng)*, He is building (a house).
U nang-tháw (íng), He is going on building (a house.)
U iai-tháw (íng), He goes on building.

With a subordinate sentence, or an adverb of *past* time, these may have the force of the past, as—

Ū dang-tháw íng mynhynnin, He was still building a house yesterday.

Mynba nga la poi, u dang tháw íng, When I arrived he was building, or, was still building a house.

PAST.—*U la dang tháw (íng)*, He was (still) building (a house).
U la nang tháw (íng), He went on building (a house).

FUTURE.—*U'n dang tháw (íng)*
U'n nang tháw (íng)
U'n iai tháw (íng)
} He will, or, shall be building (a house).

FUTURE COMPLETE.—

U'n da la dang tháw (íng) } He will, or, shall have been
U'n da la nang tháw (íng) } building (a house).

PRESENT COMPLETE.—*U wan tháw (íng)*, He has been building (a house)—*lit.*, He is come (from) building a house.

U wan thoh (díng), He has been cutting (wood).

PAST COMPLETE.—*U la lah wan tháw (íng)*, He had been building (a house).

Note 1.—This construction with *wan* (to come) is very peculiar, but quite idiomatic, and very extensive. When the phrase is used in this sense, some such questions as "Where has he been?" "What are you doing here?" are either expressed or understood.—Ans., *Nga la wan tháw íng*, I have been building a house; or *Nga la wan thoh díng*, I have been cutting wood, *lit.*, I have come (from) cutting wood.

Note 2.—The context may give it another meaning, when it is taken word for word, *Nga la wan tháw íng*, I have come to build a house. But *ba'n* should in this case be used before *tháw*, to avoid ambiguity; thus, *Nga la wan ba'n tháw íng*, or *Nga la wan ba'n thoh díng*.

Subjunctive.

PRESENT. { *Lada u dang tháw (íng)*, If he is building (a house).
Haba u da dang tháw (íng), If he be building (a house).

PRESENT.
- *Lada u nang tháw (íng)*, If he is going on building (a house).
- *Haba u da nang tháw (íng)*, If he be going on building (a house).

PAST.
- *Lada u la dang tháw (íng)*, If he was building (a house).
- *Haba u da la dang tháw (íng)*, If he were building (a house).

FUTURE.—*Haba u'n da dang tháw (íng)*, If he should be building (a house).

PRESENT COMPLETE.—*Lada u la wan tháw (íng)*, If he has been building (a house).

PAST COMPLETE.—*Lada u la lah wan tháw (íng)*, If he had been building (a house).

FUTURE COMPLETE.—*Lada u'n da la dang tháw (íng)*, If he should have been building (a house).

Potential.

PRESENT.—*Ka lah, ba nga dang tháw (íng)*, I may be building (a house).

Ka lah, ba nga nang tháw (íng), I may be going on building (a house).

PAST.—*Ka lah, ba u la dang tháw (íng)*, He might be building (a house).

Ka lah, ba u la nang tháw (íng), He might be going on building (a house).

FUTURE.—*Ka lah, ba nga'n dang tháw (íng)*, I might be building (a house). Only in Complex Sent.

Ka lah, ba nga'n nang tháw (íng), I might be going on building (a house). In Complex Sent.

PRESENT COMPLETE.—*Ka lah, ba nga la wan tháw (íng)*, I may have been building (a house).

PAST COMPLETE.—*Ka lah, ba nga la lah wan tháw (íng)*, I might have been building (a house).

Note.—The student will read again our remark on *wan* on page 97, § 69, *Indicative Mood,* after *Pres.* and *Past Complete*, which is also applicable here.

Imperative.

PRESENT.—*Tó, da nang tháw (íng)*, Go on building (a house).

Tó ái ba nga'n nang tháw (íng), Let me go on building (a house).

Tó ái ba u'n nang tháw (íng), Let him go on building (a house).

See note under § 64, *Imperative Mood,* which shows that this form is also *Future.*

Infinitive.

Ba'n dang tháw (íng), To be building (a house).
Ba'n nang tháw (íng), To go on building (a house).
Ba'n iai-tháw (íng), To continue building (a house).

INFINITIVE IN *íng*.

Kaba dang tháw (íng).
Kaba nang tháw (íng).
Kaba iai tháw (íng).

Participle.

This is expressed in Khassi by a sentence introduced by a conjunction *ba* (because), so giving it a *personal* force.

PRESENT COMPLETE.—*Ba* (*u*) *la wan tháw* (*íng*), Having been building (a house.)

Ba (*u*) *la wan khymih*, Having been seeing.

The pronoun inserted in brackets may be of any person, according to the circumstances or the sense of the context.

EXAMPLES.

(1) *Ba* (*u*) *la* WAN *shong-kulai, u sngow thait eh*, Having been riding, he is very tired.

(2) *Ba* (*nga*) *la* WAN *khymíh ia ka íng, nga'm shym lah ioh ih ia phi*, Having been seeing the house, I was not able to see you.

(3) *Ba nga la* LEIT *khymih ia la u kypá, ka íng ka la long suda*, Having been visiting my father, the (or MY) house was empty.

Note 1.—It will be observed from the above, that the form is only a *substitute* for our *Participle*, rather than an identical *participial* form.

Note 2.—The verb *leit* (to go) is also used like *wan* as an auxiliary to express an action in progression in past time, with this difference, that *wan* implies the actual presence of the person concerned, and *leit* that he is absent, as—

(1) *Mynba u iáp, u la leit tháw íng* (absent), When he died, he had been building a house.

(2) *Mynba u iáp, u la wan tháw íng* (present), When he died, he had been building a house.

PASSIVE VOICE.

Indicative Mood.

PRESENT.—*Dang tháw ia (ka íng)*, (The house) is being built.

FUTURE.—*Yn dang tháw ia (ka íng)*, (The house) will be building.

Yn nang tháw ia (ka íng), They will go on building (the house), *or* (The house) will be going on building.

PAST.—*La dang tháw ia (ka íng)*, (The house) was being built.

COMPLETE.—*La lah nang tháw ia (ka íng)*, (The house) has been building.

Subjunctive Mood.

PRESENT.—*Lada dang tháw ia (ka íng)*, If (the house) is being built.

Uncertainty:—*Haba da dang tháw ia (ka íng)*, If (the house) be building.

Haba da nang tháw ia (ka íng), If (the house) be going on building.

FUTURE.—*Lada yn nang tháw ía (ka íng)*, If (the house) will be building.

Haba'n da dang tháw ia (ka íng), If (the house) should be building.

PAST, FACT.—*Lada la dang tháw ia (ka íng)*, If (the house) was building.

Uncertainty :—*Haba da la dang tháw ia (ka íng)*, If (the house) were building.

PAST COMPLETE.—*Lada la lah nang tháw ia (ka íng)*, If the house had been building.

Potential Mood.

PRESENT.—*Ka lah, ba ki dang tháw ia (ka íng)*, The house may be building.

Lehse, ba dang tháw ia (ka íng), Perhaps the house is being built, *or* The house may be building.

FUTURE.—*Ka lah, ba ki'n da nang tháw ia (ka íng)*,
Lehse, yn nang tháw ia (ka íng),
The house might be building.

PAST.—
Ka lah, ba ki la dang tháw ia (ka íng),
Ka lah, ba la nang tháw ia (ka íng),
Lehse, ba la nang tháw ia (ka íng),
The house might be building.

COMPLETE.—
Ka lah, ba ki la lah nang tháw ia (ka íng),
Ka lah, ba la lah nang tháw ia (ka íng),
Lehse, ba la lah nang tháw ia (ka íng),
The house may *or* might have been building.

OUGHT, SHOULD.— *Ka dei, ba ki da nang tháw ia (ka íng),*
Ka dei, ba yn nang tháw ia (ka íng),

The house should *or* ought to be building.

COMPLETE.—*Ka la dei, ba ki la nang tháw ia (ka íng),*
The house should *or* ought to have been building.

Note.—We do not know of any other mode of expressing the Progressive Potential in Khassi. *Ki* (they) is used indefinitely, like our 'they' in 'they say,' i.e. 'it is said;' or the French *on* in *on dit, on parle,* &c. See § 58, 3. The force of *ka* in *ka lah* (it is possible) has already been explained and illustrated in the various paradigms.

EMPHATIC FORM.

§ 70. There is no auxiliary verb in Khassi that corresponds to our English 'do.' Emphasis is expressed by means of such adverbs as *shisha* [Beng. সত্য, سچا] (truly), *kein* (of course), *shym* (not), *put* (yet), *jiw* (ever); or by laying particular stress on the word or words to be emphasized.

Indicative Mood.

PRESENT.—*Nga ïeit* SHISHA, lit., I love INDEED=I do love.
Nga'm ïeit SHISHA, lit., I love not INDEED=I do not love.

PAST.—*Nga la ïeit* SHISHA *(ia phi)*, lit., I loved (you) INDEED=I did love (you).
Nga'm SHYM *ïeit (ia phi)*, I did not love (you).
Nga'm JIW *la ïeit (ia u)*, I NEVER DID love (him).

FUTURE.—*Nga'n ïeit* SHISHA (*ia phi*), I WILL love (you).

Nga'n ym ïeit SHUH (*ia u*), I will love (him) NO MORE.

§ 71. These emphatic particles are often employed together; such as *shym* and *shuh*, *put* and *shym*, *jiw* and *shuh*, thus:—

U'm SHYM *wan shuh*, lit., He DID not come AGAIN=He never came.

U'm PUT *shym wan*, lit., He has not yet come=He HAS not come.

U'm JIW *wan shuh*, lit., He NEVER comes AGAIN=He never comes.

§ 72. *Shym* and *put* are used *exclusively* in negative sentences, and the former expresses past time; *jiw* and *shuh* are not necessarily negative, as maintained by some. (There is a 'shuh' which answers to our 'stop!' 'keep away!' 'hands off!') These are always emphatic but not necessarily negative. The literal meaning of *shuh* is 'again,' 'any more.'

Phi'n wan SHUH? Will you come AGAIN?

Phi'n ym wan SHUH? You will not come AGAIN?

Ai soh SHUH *ia nga*, Give me MORE fruit.

Wat wan SHUH *shane*, Do not come here ANY MORE.

ADDITIONAL REMARKS ON THE VERBS, MOODS, AND TENSES.

§ 73. The verbs *long* and *don* should be distinguished. *Long* expresses existence generally and absolutely, as when we speak of God.

U Bleí U long, God is, *or* God exists.

Or 'to become,' as when we speak of plants taking root—

Ki jinthung ki la long, The plants have taken root.

Ka jingiaseng ka la long, The meeting has taken place, or has commenced.

Or, it is used very commonly as a descriptive verb—

Ka Ktín ka long Bleí, The Word is God.

U Bleí U long U babhá, God is good.

On the other hand, *don* denotes either simply 'to be'—

U Briw u don ha íng, The man is in the house.

U Bleí U don, There is a God.

Or, *don* is often used transitively, for 'to have'—

U sím u don bún spah, The king has much wealth.

From the above examples it will be observed, that the distinction between these two verbs of existence does not exactly correspond to that between হওন and আছি in Bengali, the latter being defective; for *long*, unlike হওন, is *regularly* used as a descriptive, while *don* is exclusively confined to expressing the idea of simple existence (to be) and that of possession (to have).

§ 74. The form for the *Past Indefinite* with *la* simply, is often used to express the *Present Complete*, as—

Quest. Phi la thoh? for *Phi la lah thoh?* Have you written?

Ans. Haoid, nga la thoh mynhynnin, Yes, I wrote yesterday.

Or, *Haoid, nga la thoh*, Yes, I *have* written.

§ 75. The form *la lah* is the *Present Complete* when used in a simple sentence complete in itself, as—

Nga la lah thoh ia ka shitti, I *have written* the letter.

But in a compound or complex sentence, with the subordinate sentence or clause in the past tense, *la lah* has the force of the *Past Complete,* as—

Nga la lah thoh ia ka shitti, mynba u la poi, I *had written* the letter, when he arrived.

§ 76. Sentences introduced by *lada* ('if') are suppositions of a *fact,* but those introduced by *haba* followed by *da* are suppositions of an *uncertainty.* After the former class of subordinate clauses, the *Past Indefinite* form of the *Indicative* has often the force of the *Past Complete* of the *Potential* Mood, thus—

Lada nga la lah don hangta, u la kren *ia ka bashisha,* If I had been there, he *would have spoken* the truth.

The principal clause or *apodosis* here might be written thus—

U'n da la lah kren ia ka bashisha, He would have spoken the truth.

Doubt in either of the clauses would require the form with *da,* thus—

Lada nga la lah don hangta, u'n da *la kren shái,* If I had been there, he *might have* spoken plainly.

Haba *nga* da *la lah don hangtá, ka lah ba u'n da la kren shái,* If I had been *or* were there, he *might have* spoken plainly.

The native student should pay particular attention to the essential difference between a subjunctive with *lada*, and one introduced by *haba-da*, when writing, translating, or conversing in English. The comparatively small progress which they have hitherto made in speaking and writing correct English, is mainly due to lack of diligence in rendering and distinguishing the various moods, *e.g.*

(1) *Lada u'n wan*, If he comes, *or* If he will come.

(2) *Haba u da wan*, Should he come, *or* If he should come.

§ 77. The *y* in *shym* (not) should be pronounced like the French *u* in *une*, or like the *y* in *Tyndal*. See § 6, and Prefatory Remarks to the "Anglo-Khassi Dictionary" page iv.

§ 78. When the particle *dang* follows the other auxiliaries *lá* or *la lah* in the various tense formations, it should be itself considered as an auxiliary. But when *dang* precedes these auxiliaries, it is a simple adverb, meaning 'just;' as—

(1) *U la dang tháw ia ka íng* (progressive form), He was building the house.

(2) *U dang lah tháw ia ka íng* (used adverbially), He has *just* finished the house.

U dang la kren mynta ha nga, He has *just* spoken (now) to me.

§ 79. The verb *ioh* (to have) is often used as an auxiliary instead of *lah* (to be able) to express some forms of the Potential Mood, as—

(1) *Nga'n ioh wan,* I shall come=I will be able to come.

(2) *Nga'm ioh wan,* I shall not come=I cannot come.

(3) *U'n ym ioh wan,* He shall not come; equal to *U'n ym lah wan,* He will not be able to come.

CHAPTER VII.

The Adverb.

§ 80. Definition.—Adverbs qualify *attributes,* that is, *Verbs, Adjectives,* or other *Adverbs,* as—U saheb u la *kylli byniah eh,* The gentleman enquired *very* minutely. Here *byniah* qualifies the verb *kylli,* and *eh* (very) the adverb *byniah.*

Examples.

(1) Qualifying *Verbs.*—U la poi *mynta,* He arrived *to-day.*

U thïah *khop,* He sleeps *soundly.*

U kren *shái,* He speaks *distinctly.*

(2) Qualifying *Adj.*—Kane ka long kháin *eh,* This is *very* coarse.

U long ba la iaroh *kylleng,* He is *universally praised.*

Kane ka kam ka long sniw *naduh-haduh,* This business is wrong *altogether.* Lit., This business is wrong *from one end to the other.*

(3) Qualifying *Adv.*—U iáid *kham* jem, He walks *more* easily.

U briw u la ïaid stet *katta*, The man walked *so* fast.

Ka la kren adykar *khyndiat*, She spoke guardedly *rather*.

§ 81. The Khassi language is very rich in *Adverbs*, and in the case of those mentioned under Classes 2 and 3, they may be considered, many of them, to belong to the untranslatables of the language. When the highest or lowest degree of any quality is often expressed in English by the generic adverb 'very,' the Khassis never want a *specific* which at once suggests the object or quality meant. Thus '*very* yellow' is rendered '*stem* LYMIED-LYMIED;' '*very* red'=*sáw* HAIN-HAIN. When the adverb *dik-dik* (faintly) is used with the verb *padia* (to beat), it is at once known that it refers to the heart beating faintly near death; when the adjective *sngáid* (fat) is qualified by *lykoi* (sleeky), it refers to very small animals of their class; *lykui*, to short-legged beasts, such as the pig; *lykhur-lykhur* is applied only to fat babies; *lykhung* (motionless) with *ngat* (to fall), always refers to cows or oxen falling, when about to be slaughtered; *lybuit* with *lyngkhuid* (naked), refers to aged persons devoid of clothing; *lybait*, on the other hand, always refers to children, and means in all these cases 'very' or 'entirely' or 'stark' naked. Again, a great number of adverbs are used with the verb *snoh* (to hang) according to the size, shape or manner, all of which are suggested by the adverb used. Thus *snoh-lyján* would imply that the object is hanging down loosely. In the same way a great number of adverbs follow the verb *khih* (to move), as *khih doi-doi, khih dob-dob, khih mop-mop, khih krib krib.*

1. Adverbs of Time.

§ 82. (1) Adverbs denoting past time mostly take the prefix *myn-*, 'ago.'

mynta, to-day, now.
mynstep, in the morning.
mynhynne, just now.
mynhynnin, yesterday.
mynmïeit, at night.
mynnore, a short time ago.
mynno? when?
mynno-mynno, formerly.
mynno-mynno-ruh, ever.
myn-arïa, two days ago.
mynariew, a fortnight ago.
mynsngi, noon, at noon.
mynwei, in former times.
mynumwei, the year before last.
myn-sawïa, four days ago.
myn-shisngi, day before yesterday.
mynkata, then.
mynshiwa, formerly, before.
mynhyndai, in old times.
mynkulong, in the remote past.
mynnyngkong, at first.
mynsynia, at midnight.
myndang, while, when.
myn-dang-long, at the beginning.
mynpyrhem, in the hot season.
mynlýur, in the wet season.
mynsynrai, in summer.
myntylang, in winter.
mynhynne-mynmïeit, last night.

mynhynne-mynsngi, at noon to-day.

mynhynne-mynstep, this morning.

mynhynnin-mynsngi, mid-day yesterday.

mynhynnin-mynmïeit, yesternight.

mynshi-snem, a year ago.

mynár-snem, two years ago.

(2) Adverbs denoting *futurity* take the prefix *la*, as—

lashái, to-morrow.

las'it, just now, in the evening.

lashibit, presently.

lashisngi, day after to-morrow.

lano? when?

lawei, in future, next year.

lano-lano, at some future time.

lano-lano-ruh, ever.

With the negative *ém*=*lano-lano-ruh-ém*, 'never.'

(3) *La* sometimes expresses *past time*, but with a different meaning to that of *myn*, as—

la arsngi, since two days.
la mynwei, since last year.
la katta ruh, after so long.
la arsín, twice gone.

(4) Adverbs denoting *repetition* take *man*='every,' (fr. '*man*' to grow, arise, or become), as—

man ka sngi, daily.

man ta iew, weekly.

man-bynai, *man u bynai*, } monthly.

man ka mïeit, nightly.

man ka step, every morning.

man ka snem, yearly.

Ha la is used in the same way, as—

ha la ka sngi, every day.
ha la shitaiew, every week.
ha la bynái, every month.
ha la ka'rta, always, perpetually, for ever, eternally.
ha la ka snem, yearly.
ha la miëit, nightly.
ha la ka step, every morning.
iai-, prefix denoting repetition or persistence.

(5) Other Adverbs of time:—

shen, soon.
shen-shen, very soon.
shen-shen, in rapid succession.
shuh, again, any more.
artat, at the same time.
kumne, presently, now.
kumne-kumne, immediately, in close succession.
katta, so long, after so long.
kloi, soon.
kloi-kloi, very soon, in rapid succession.
bïang, again, once more.
katto-katne, for a while.
katba, as long as, whilst.
bún-sín, often.
dang, yet, still, just.
dàk, at once.
haba, when, after (*lit.*, in that).
haba-dei, sometimes, occasionally.
haba-dei-badei, now and then.
eh, often (*lit.*, very).
hadín, after, afterwards.
haduh, until.
haduh-katno? How long?
hynda (historical), when, after.
haduh lano? until when?
ha shiwa, before.
habynda, until.
hamar, when (simultaneity.)
poh-ïa, immaturely, before the time.
shiwád, once.

shisintokhat, once in a way.
shi-syndon, at once, without delay.
shiphang, firstly, in or for a short time.
shi-kyntin, once.
satïa, at all.
ym-satïa, not at all.
shisin, once.
junom, ever, everlastingly.
jiw, ever, habitually.
jindei, continually.
jang-jang, very soon.
mynsynïa-mynsngi, night and day, incessantly.
lajan-mïeit, in the evening.
naduh, since.
naduh-haduh, always.
nadín, after.
nang-, prefix denoting simultaneity.
pat, again.
pat-pa-pat, again and again.
roit-roit, in quick succession.
roit-pa-roit, repeatedly.
rúing, back on same day.
putsngi, every alternate day.
sa katto-katne, after a while.
baroh-shi-katta, all along.
baroh-shi-lynti, all along.
baroh-shi-lynter, all along.
ha teng, sometimes.
ha teng-ha teng, now and then.
ynda-hadín-pat, afterwards.
ryngkat, at the same time.
-sin, suffix=times.
shi-sin, once.
arsin, twice.
laisin, thrice, &c., &c.
-wád, suffix=times.
arwád, twice, &c.
habadei, sometimes.
habadei-badei, occasionally.

2. Adverbs of Manner.

adykar, prudently, carefully.
artatin, doubtingly.
bhá, well.
bhúk, suddenly.
bhúk-bhák, confusedly.

bïang, rightly, justly.
bein, scornfully.
brop, unexpectedly.
brein-brein, in spots.
byniah, exactingly.
bynnud, scrupulously, a-grumbling.
b'ymman, wickedly.
biriah, jokingly.
bak, briskly.
balei? why? *ym-balei?* why not?
bor, forcibly, by force.
káw-káw, noisily.
kein, of course.
khong-khong, peevishly, angrily.
khrup, lowly, humbly.
khop, soundly.
khráw, proudly, haughtily.
khram, with a crash.
khong-pong, headlong.
khák, closely, tightly.
khnang, purposely.
katba-kynduh, at random.
khyndiat, rather.
kylláin, in a round-about way, evasively.
kylláin-kyrjáw, wanderingly.
kynjoh, ambitiously, take-all, arrogantly.
kynthïap, humbly, lowly.
kynbrum-kynbram, topsy-turvy.
kynrum-kynram, topsy-turvy.
kyntïak, nimbly.
kynneng, motionless.
kynjah, lonely, desolately.
kymang, agape, expectantly.
kyntung, conspicuously.
kynshiriang, elegantly, with airs, gaudily, gracefully.
kynjai, happily, cosily.
kyrhái, abundantly.
kumno? how?
kumno-kumno-ruh, any how.
kumno-ruh-kumno, somehow or another.
kumne, thus, in this way.
kumta, so, in that way.
kwïah-kwïah, weakly.
dang shú . . . , scarcely, hardly.

doi-doi, dingle-dangle.
dik-dik, faintly.
dob-dob, loosely.
dór, distortedly.
dáw-dáw, noisily.
duh-sngi, at a loss.
duh-ei, to no purpose.
de, too.
da kumwei, otherwise.
da-lei-lei-ruh, on any account.
da-la-de-hí, of one's own accord.
ei, freely, gratuitously.
eh, very, harshly, hard, greatly.
hár-hár, pleasantly.
háin-háin, like crimson.
hèr-hèr, pleasantly.
hin, sweetly.
hìr-hìr, eagerly.
hí, alone, by oneself.
hók (حق), rightly, justly.
hor-hor, awfully.
hún, soothingly.
ia-, pref. den. mutually.
jár-jár, quietly, secretly.
jir-jir, quietly, secretly.
jin, almost.
jindei, entirely.
jem, mildly, smoothly.
joit, suddenly, nimbly, up.
jai, calmly, quietly.
jew-sẹw, surly, bitterly.
-lin, to the brim.
lím, on the back.
'let, amiss, unintentionally.
lang, together.
láin-láin, wavingly.
leng, all round, conspicuously.
mïan-mïan, slowly, softly.
mop-mop, with a twitch.
marwei, alone.
markylliang, mutually.
mar-ryngkat, together.
noh-ei, in vain, to nothing.
niun, poorly.
ngeng, heavily.
ngúr-ngúr, indistinctly.
ngér-ngér, indistinctly.
ngír-ngír, indistinctly.
ngut-ngut, } dimly.
ngẹt-ngẹt, }
ngoi-ngoi, weakly.
phar, entirely, quite.

phit, entirely, in a mass.
phak-phak, violently.
poh, lowly, humbly, meanly.
prak, precisely, to the mark.
puh-hái, wastefully.
pahuh-hái, wastefully.
-phái, backwards.
pyrshah, against, in opposition.
rít, lowly, humbly.
rïang-rïang, in a row, orderly, seriatim.
ryngmang, unexpectedly, from no apparent cause.
rynghang, ajar.
rynjung, in a cluster or bunch.
ryngkhat, suddenly.
sa khyndiat, nearly, almost, within a little.
sak, straightway.
sa, discontentedly.
s'am, grudgingly.
sàm, keenly.
sakïat, evidently.
salïa, discontentedly.
sah, permanently.
shikkadei, exceedingly.
skhem, fast, firmly, positively.
shalai, deceitfully.
shái, clearly, distinctly.
soit, suddenly, abruptly.
slait, closely.
slak, tightly.
shù, merely, only.
stád, wisely, prudently.
stet, quickly.
sníw, badly, wickedly, ill.
tèr-tèr, in order.
tain-tain, violently, harshly.
thàn, prodigally, liberally.
tém-tém, lazily.
wàr, entirely.
wang, wide open.
tam, too much.

Note.—The prefix *-ia* has the force of our suffix *-ly* in many cases, as *ia-rykhie*, 'laughingly.'

3. Adverbs of Place.

arsut, downwards.
artet, upwards.
dadín, backwards.
dín, backwards.
kyrtiang, backwards.
kylleng, everywhere.

kyrphang, apart.
kyrphong, behind.
Ha, in.
Haei? Where?
haei-haei-ruh, anywhere.
haei-ruh-haei, somewhere (unknown).
haei-haei-ruh-ém, nowhere.
hangno? (*ha-kano?*) where?
hangno-h.-ruh, anywhere.
hangno-h.-ruh-ém, nowhere.
hangno-ruh-hangno, somewhere (unknown).
hangne-bad-shawei, here and there.
hawei-bad-shawei, in all directions.
ha kyndong, aside.
ha khymat, in front, before.
halor, above.
halyndet, aside (and beyond).
hangne (*ha-kane*), here.
hangta (*ha-kata*), there.
hangtai (*ha-katai*), there.
hangto (*ha-kato*), there.
hakyrphong, behind.
ha shiwa, before, in front.
hasyndah, beside.
hajan, near.
lajan, almost.
lyngeh, sidewise.
marjan, close to.
markhap, near, adjacent.
mar-ryngkat, equal, together.
mar-pyrshah, over against.
mar-pyrdih, half-way.
mar-pyddeng, in the middle.
mar-khymat, before; face to face.
naei? where from?
naei-naei-ruh, whencesoever.
naei-naei-ruh-ém, from nohere.
naei-ruh-naei, from somewhere.
nangne, hence.
nangta, thence (*na-kata*).
nangtai, thence (*na-katai*).
nangto, thence (*na-kato*).
nangno? Where from?
nangno-n-ruh, whencesoever.
nangno-ruh-nangno, from somewhere.
nalor, from above.

napoh, from below or within.
nabár (fr. B. বাহির, or H. باهر), from without.
noh, away, off.
-pyrshíng, side-long.
-pyllup, with face downwards.
sha, to (motion).
shaei? where to.
shaei-shaei-ruh, anywhere.
shaei-shaei-ruh-ém, nowhere.
shaei-ruh-shaei, somewhere.
shalor, above.
shabar, out, abroad.
sha lyngam, abroad (foreign).
sha nongwei, from home.
shadín, behind, after.
sha shiwa, in the front, ahead.
sha-lyndet, aside, beyond.
sha kïar, aside, alongside.
sawdong, round about.
shane (*sha-kane*), here.
shano? (*sha-kano?*) Where to?
shano-shano-ruh, anywhere.
shano-shano-ruh-ém, nowhere.
shano-ruh-shano, somewhere.
shata, yonder (out of sight).
shatai, yonder (at a great distance).
shato, yonder (in sight).
shathí, to the south, that is, downwards, because the south is towards the plains.
sharum, below, underneath.
sybak, backwards.

Note.—For the force of the Adverbs composed of *kata*, *katai*, *kato*, &c., see under the Demonstrative Pronouns.

4. Adverbs of Affirmation and Negation, &c.

Kein, of course.
dú, really, indeed.
adé, perchance.
ni, indeed.
ém, no, not.
se, indeed, to be sure.
ym, not.
ym . . . dalei? Why not?

haoid, yes.
niuma, very well, all right.
lehse, perhaps.
da-lei-lei-ruh-ém, on no account.
koit, all right.
shisha (سچا), certainly.
ym . . . heit? Why not?
ym . . . satïa, not at all.

CHAPTER VIII.

The Preposition.

§ 83. Prepositions are words *placed before* nouns or pronouns to show the relation in which they stand to some other word in the sentence, as—

Ka íng *jong* nga, The house OF me=MY house.

U briw *halor* íng, The man ON the house.

It will be observed that many of the words to be here registered as Prepositions have already been classed under the Adverbs. The distinction rests on this, that the Prepositions always precede and govern some Noun or its equivalent, expressed or understood.

§ 84. *Classification.*—Like Adverbs, Prepositions express relations of *Place* and *Time;* they also express *Agency, Cause, Intention, Opposition,* &c.

PREPOSITIONS OF PLACE.

ha, in, to.
hadín, after, behind.
haduh, up to, to, as far as.
hawei, elsewhere.
hajan, near.
halor, above, on, upon.

haphang, by or at the side (of).
hamar, about, near.
haphrang, before, in front (of).
hapoh, within, in.
hapyddeng, between, in the middle.
harúd, at or by the side (of).
harum, below.
hashiwa, before.
ha khymat, before.
ha jerong, on the top (of).
ha kyrphong, behind.
kylleng, about.
jan, near.
na, from.
nabar, out of, from outside.
najan, from near.
napoh, from within.
nalor, from the top of, besides.
nadín, after, from behind.
nadúh, from.
lyngbah, through.
lyndet, beyond.
shaphang, towards.
sharum, below.
narúd, from the side.
narúd-sharúd, athwart.
mar-ḳhymat, before, opposite.
mar-pyrshah, opposite, over against.
mar-jan, close to.
pynkhïang, across.
pyrshah, opposite, against.
narum, from below.
sha, to (motion to).
shabar, outside.
shalor, on the top.
shaneng, on the top.
sha shiliang, across.
shapoh, within.

Prepositions of Time.

naduh, since.
hapyddeng, during.
haduh, until.
jin, about.
ha, at.
hamar, about.
ia, during.
kumba, about, thereabout.

The prefix *myn*, noticed under the Adverbs, was originally a preposition denoting time—*in*, as *myn-step*=in the morning.

PREPOSITIONS OF AGENCY.

bad, with.

da, by, through, by means of.

DENOTING CAUSE.

namar, because, for.

namar jong, for the sake of, on account of.

na ka bynta jong, for the sake of.

ia, for, to.

OTHER RELATIONS.

khlem, without, except.

ha ka jaka jong, instead of.

pyrshah, against.

katba-kum, according to.

shaphang, concerning.

jong, of.

ia, against.

khnang ia, for.

CHAPTER IX.

The Conjunction.

§ 85. *Conjunctions* join words, clauses, or sentences, as—

Ma-u *bad* ma-phi, He AND you.

Nga la wan, *namar* ba phi la wan, I came BECAUSE you came.

§ 86. *Classification.*—Conjunctions are either *Copulative, Disjunctive,* or *Correlative.*

§ 87. *The Copulative Conjunctions* not only grammatically connect words or sentences, but also the meaning which those words and sentences convey.

ba, that, because, since.
bad, and.
kat, as, so, like.
katba, like as, as.
kum, like.
kumba, as.
kumta, so.
kumjuh, likewise, so, as.
de, also, even.
ia, than.
leh', perhaps.
lehse, perhaps.
lada, if.
la', though, although.
mynba, whilst.
mynba kumta, in the meanwhile.
nangta, hence.
nalor kane, besides, moreover.
namar kata, therefore.
naba, since, whereas.
pat, further, again.
ynda, after.
ynda kumta, after that.
ynda hadín, subsequently.
ynda hadín pat, after, again.
té, then, but.
tadynda, until, till after.
tang ba, only that . . . .
ynda slem, after a long while.

§ 88. *Disjunctive Conjunctions,* whilst they grammatically connect words or sentences, logically *dis*join them.

l'ymda, except, save.
lane, either, or.
ne, or.
l'ymne, nor.
la', though.
pynban, yet, nevertheless.

la' katno-katno-ruh, however so much.
hinrei, but.
le, but.
tang, except, only.
la'kata ruh, yet, still.
la'kumta ruh, yet, still.
la' kumno-kumno-ruh, anyhow.

§ 89. *Correlative Conjunctions* are those which suggest, or answer to, one another, as—

(1)	*katba* ...	... *kumta* }	as	so.
(2)	*kumba*...	... *kumta* }		
(3)	*kumba*...	... *kumjuh*	as	so.
(4)	*katta* ...	... *ba*	{ so	that.
			{ so	as.
(5)	*lane* ...	... *lane*	either ...	or.
(6)	*lymne* ...	... *lymne*	neither ...	nor.
(7)	*bad* ...	... *bad*	both ...	and.
(8)	*la'* ...	... *pynban*	though ...	yet.
(9)	*ym tang*	... *hinrei*	not only ...	but.
(10)	*la'* ...	... *ne*	whether ...	or.

EXAMPLES.

(1) *Katba* u la nang pynih, *kumta* hí ka la jïa, As he was explaining, so indeed it happened.

(2 *Kumba* phi la ong, *kumta* hí ka long, As you said, so indeed it is.

(3) *Kumba* phi pynih, *kumjuh* ruh nga hí nga sngow, As you show, so indeed I feel myself.

(4) Ka la shit *katta, ba* u'm lah shong shuh, It was so hot, THAT he could no longer stay.

(5) U Sím u'n pyddiang *lane* ia phi, *lane* u kypa jong

phi, The king will receive EITHER you OR your father.

Lane u'n ïh-sih ia uwei, *lane* u'n ïeit ia uwei pat, He will EITHER hate the one, OR love the other.

(6) U'm íhthuh *lymne* ia phi, *lymne* ia u kypa jong phi, He knows NEITHER you, NOR your father.

(7) Ngi'n ialeit, *bad* ma-u, *bad* ma-nga de, We will go, BOTH he AND I.

(8) *La'* u'm don tyngka hí, *pynban* u nang pynlut, ALTHOUGH he has no money himself, YET he goes on spending.

(9) *Ym tang* ba u sníw, *hinrei* ba u'm tip ei-ei, NOT ONLY because he is bad, BUT also because he knows nothing.

(10) *La'* u long sím, *ne* u 'ríw kyrduh, nga'm sngow phér, WHETHER he be a king, OR a poor man, it makes no difference to me.

CHAPTER X.

The Interjection.

§ 90. Interjections are words which express some passion, such as joy, grief, admiration, encouragement, warning, &c.

Adur! Ow! Oh! Ah!
Adur-ba'n shot! Away!
Adí! Oh, dear! Oh, my!
Ado! Ho-ho!
Ade! May be!
Káw! Hurrah!
Ko! My! Hé!
Ko lók! My friend!
Gíw! Tush!
Líh! Friend!
Khublei! Adieu! Welcome! God bless you! God speed!
Máp ianga! Excuse me!
Waw! Oh, heaven!
Shi! O fie!
Shish! Pooh!
Shisha! Indeed! True!
Sngáp! Listen!
Ià! Let us be off!
Sumar! Take care!
Tó! All right!
Wáw Mei! Oh, mother!

PART III.

SYNTAX.

Introductory Remarks on Arrangement.

§ 91. The Nominative, which may be a noun or a pronoun (*u, ka, ki*), generally *precedes* the verb, as—

U briw, u la iám, The man (he) wept.

Ka íng, ka la kyllon, The house (it) fell.

Ka wah, ka'n ryngád, The river (it) will dry up.

§ 92. For the sake of *emphasis,* however, the nominative often *follows* its verb, as—

U la *iám,* or La *iám* u briw, The man WEPT.

La *wan* u briw, The man CAME.

§ 93. In interrogative sentences emphasis is marked more by the tone of the voice than by the arrangement of the parts.

U kulai u la *iap ?* Is the horse DEAD ?

U *kulai* u la *iap ?* Is the HORSE dead ?

La *kyllon* ka íng ? Has the house FALLEN ?

La kyllon ka *íng ?* Has the HOUSE fallen ?

§ 94. The Object generally *follows* the verb.

U Sím u la leit sïat *sim,* The king is gone a bird-shooting.

U Sím u sïat *sim,* The king shoots BIRDS.

U Sìm u puh *kybá,* The bird pecks GRAIN.

Ka samla ka kit *díng,* The lass (she) carries WOOD.

§ 95. For the sake of *emphasis* the object sometimes *precedes* the verb, as—

Ia u soh, u la lah díe, He HAS sold the oranges.

Ia *la ka kymi,* u'm ïeit, He does not love his OWN MOTHER.

§ 96. *Adjectives* follow the nouns they qualify, as—

Ka massi *basngáid,* A FAT COW.

U lúm *bajerong,* A HIGH mountain.

U khynnah *basïan,* A CUNNING boy.

U khún *batipsngi,* A GOOD child.

U briw *bahok,* u ïeit ia U Blei, A RIGHTEOUS man loves God.

U kulai u kit ia u briw *baheh,* The horse carries a BIG man.

§ 97. When the adjective seems to precede the noun, it in reality follows the pronoun (*u* or *ka*) which stands for the noun, according to the rule given. Such phrases are always elliptical sentences having the verb *long* (is) understood, as—

U *babhá* u briw—lit., He (is) GOOD, the man = He is a GOOD man.

U *baheh* u kulai—lit., It (is) BIG, the horse = It is a BIG horse.

The adjectives in such phrases are always emphatic. See § 35, Note 4, and § 110 (2).

§ 98. Except when *emphasis* requires a different arrangement, Adverbs *follow* the words they modify:

U la iáp *mynta,* He died TO-DAY.

U'n wan *las'it,* He will come IN THE EVENING.

U sim u la hér *noh,* The bird is flown AWAY.

Ka jáin ka la iong *ngain,* The cloth has become JET black.

U soh u byrthïang *khyndiat,* The fruit is a LITTLE sweetish.

Interrogative Adverbs may either precede or follow the verb:

Na-ei phi wan? Phi wan *na-ei*?	Where do you come from?
Shano phi leit? Phi leit *shano*?	Where are you going?
Haei phi *shong*? Phi *shong* haei?	Where do you live?

But when the adverb is to be emphasized, it should precede the verb and the nominative, thus—

Mynta u la iáp, It was TO-DAY he died.

La'sit u'n wan, It is IN THE EVENING he will come.

§ 99. Some adverbs have become mere suffixes, used only as integral parts of certain verbs, or classes of verbs, as—

ïeng-*joit,* To rise SUDDENLY.

mih-*soit,* To move OFF.

leh-*meng*, To act ARROGANTLY.
thïah-*khop*, To sleep SOUNDLY.
shong-*khop*, To sit DOWN.

Of the Various Kinds of Sentences.

§ 100. The SIMPLE SENTENCE has only one finite verb.

(1) This verb may be intransitive, and the sentence will then consist of only a *Subject* and *Predicate*.

U sìm u hér, The bird flies.
U sím u synshàr, The king rules.
Ka mynsím ka la jàh, The, or, my breath is gone.

(2) Or the verb may be transitive, when the sentence consists of a Subject, Predicate, and an Object.

U ksew u bám doh, The dog eats flesh.
U khlá u la kem briw, The tiger has seized a man.

§ 101. The COMPOUND SENTENCE consists of two or more simple sentences, connected by conjunctions, which are co-ordinate to each other.

U ksew u wïar baroh shi mïet, *bad* ka mïáw ka pah, The dog barks all the night long, AND the cat mews.

U sìm-tung u symphúid ia ki khún, *te* u sír u bám ia ki, The blackbird caresses its young, BUT the stag devours them.

U khynnah u kynplom ia ka úm, *bad* ki'm lah khwái, The lad disturbs the water, so they cannot fish.

§ 102. The parts of a Compound Sentence in the *language of divination* are not connected by a conjunction.

Nga noh, nga weng (*ia u kháw*), I cast (*and*) I pick up again (the rice).

Nga pyntang, nga pynsmái, I consecrate (these) (*and*) swear (by them).

§ 103. In a COMPLEX SENTENCE, one or more of the simple sentences it may contain, are *dependent* on the *Principal Clause;* and this dependence is marked by the connecting conjunction, such as *namar*, 'because,' *ba*, 'that,' 'because,' *naba*, 'since,' &c., &c.

Ka páw bïang *ba* mé la sníw-eh, It is clear enough THAT you have become very bad.

La tei pat ia ka íng *ba* la kyllon, The house THAT fell down is rebuilt.

Ki mrád ki la íh bein ia ka ksew, *ba* ka la die ia ka ktung, The beasts despised the dog, BECAUSE it sold vetches.

Kumta u Blei u la tháw ia u briw jin árwád láiwád, *ba* u ksúid u shù dem wan prá thïaw, So God had to create man several times, BECAUSE the demon kept coming to destroy him.

Naduh ba phi wan, nga la pang eh, SINCE you came I have been very ill.

U la wan kái sha ngi, *hadin ba* phi la mih noh, He came to see us AFTER you went away.

§ 104. When the verbs in the various clauses of a

Complex Sentence have the *same* subject, the subject is expressed only in the principal clause; as,

Haba dang lah tháw la ka íng, kumno *ngi'n* thíed ia kane? Now that we have just finished a house of our own, how can WE buy this one?

CHAPTER I.

The Article.

§ 105. There is every reason to believe that the Article in Khassi was originally strictly definite. For,—

(1) It is often used without a noun expressed, in which case it has the force of a Demonstrative as well as that of a simple Personal Pronoun; as,

U la wan mynta, HE came to-day.

Ka la iap mynhynnin, SHE died yesterday.

(2) The Demonstratives are formed from the articles, *u, ka, ki*; as,

Une u'm lah kren, THIS (man) cannot speak.

Katai ka'm lah kren, THAT (woman) cannot speak.

(3) The article is often omitted when *indefiniteness* is to be expressed; as,

Úm, ym don, There is no WATER.

U sím u iaid *lúm*, The chief roams on (the) MOUNTAIN.

§ 106. The determinate sense of the article has in many instances, however, disappeared.

Ka khlíng la rong-noh ia ka doh.

This may be rendered either definitely or indefinitely, according to the circumstances at the time; thus,

A kite carried away the meat, *or* THE kite carried away the meat.

U briw la pyniap ia la u kypá, A man killed his own father, *or* THE man killed his own father.

It appears that the Khassis formerly (*as they still often do*) used the adjunct *uwei*, or *kawei*, 'one,' after the noun to express indefiniteness; thus,

U briw *uwei* u la pyniap ia la u kypá.

But in many instances this word is now dropped, except when indefiniteness is to be particularly pointed at; as,

U sím uwei u dang iáp, A king is just dead.

U sím uwei-ruh-uwei u dang-iáp, Some king or another has just died.

Hence the want of grammatical distinction between the definite and indefinite forms.

§ 107. The article is therefore *generally* used before the nominative, and again repeated before the verb.

(1) *U* khún *u* lah ba'n ih-sih ia la u kypá, THE son (he) may hate his own father.

(2) *Ka* snïang, *ka* la thár ia ka jain, THE sow (it) has torn the cloth.

(3) *Ka* mïáw *ka* pah, THE cat (it) mewls.

Note.—The article thus repeated has often the force of a Personal Pronoun used demonstratively; hence the effect of the repetition is to render the article definite in this construction.

§ 108. Before and after certain Intransitive Verbs the article is omitted, when the noun is indefinite ; as,

Don soh shibún ha kypér, There is much fruit in the garden.

Briw ym don ha íng, There is no one at home.

Ym ih don phan, shuh ha iew, There are no potatoes at all in the market it seems.

§ 109. When the article is *not* repeated before the verb, whatever be the arrangement, the noun may be taken indefinitely ; as,

La iáp ka massi, A cow is dead.

La úr u briw, A man fell.

Yn poi ki nong kitnong, Coolies will arrive.

But when the article is repeated before the verb the noun should be definite.

Ka la iap ka massi, THE cow is dead.

U la úr u briw, THE man fell.

Ki'n poi ki nong kitnong, THE coolies will come.

§ 110. THE ARTICLE BEFORE ADJECTIVES. (1) When the adjective *follows* its noun, the article may be either repeated or omitted before it.

(1) *U mrád u barúnar,* } A cruel beast.
U mrád barúnar, }

(2) *U ksew u badait eh,* } A snappish dog.
U ksew badait eh, }

(2) When the adjective *precedes* its noun it always takes the article, and the noun is *definite.* But the

adjective itself is predicative and emphatic, the verb (*long*) being understood; as,

U barúnar u ksew, The dog (is) fierce, It (is) a fierce dog.

U badait u ksew, The dog (is) snappish, It (is) a snappish dog.

Note.—When the form *ba dait u ksew, ba rúnar u ksew* occurs, *ba* is then a conjunction meaning *because*.

(See Chapter III., §§ 156, 157.)

111. Before the names of prominent objects, and monadic nouns, the article is definite, whether it be repeated or not.

(1) *La phah wád u Sím ia phi*, The king has sent for you.

(2) *Yn long ka iew la shái*, The market will be to-morrow.

(3) *Yn sa ing ka khláw la shibit*, The jungle will be on fire presently.

(4) *Ka sngi ka la mih la slem*, The sun is up long ago.

(5) *U la wan khein-ksúid u lyngdoh*, The priest is come to consult the demons.

§ 112. When the article is omitted either before the nominative or the objective case, the noun in both cases is used indefinitely; as,

(1) *Sím u'm long*, He is not a king.

Khláw don hangne, There is jungle here.

But *U sím u don hangne*, The king is here.

Ka khláw ka long hangne, The jungle is here.

(2) U la pynlong *sím* ia nga, He made me A KING.

U saheb u niew *briw* ia nga, The gentleman considers me A MAN.

Ka rukom ka shnong ka pynlong *mrád* ia u khynnah, The habits of the village make AN ANIMAL of the lad.

§ 113. When a noun forming the predicate refers the nominative to a class indefinitely, the article is then omitted before the predicate; as,

Ka Ktín ka la long *Blei,* The Word was GOD. (Jo. i. 1)

Ka ktín jong Mé ka long *jingshisha,* Thy word is TRUTH.

U Blei u long *jingïeit,* God is LOVE.

Kata ba la khá na ka doh, ka long *doh,* That which is born of the flesh is FLESH.

Note 1.—This important rule has been overlooked in the Khassi version of the New Testament, if not recently revised. In the first example, taken from Jo. i. 1, the attribute of Divinity only is asserted of Christ; although, as stated in the preceding clause, not identical with the Father, *ὁ Θεός, the God.*

Note 2.—In this version the Khassi article is treated as if *never* definite; for, to emphasize such words as *ὁ θεός, ὁ λόγος, τὸ φῶς, ἡ ἀλήθεια, ἡ ζωὴ,* &c., the relative pronoun is *added* as a substitute for the Greek article wherever it occurs in the original. This is certainly not sanctioned by either grammar or usage. In *doubtful* cases, the use of the Dem. Pronoun would be more in harmony with the genius of the language, without departing too much from literal exactness.

Note 3.—*Ktín* (word), like *parole* in French, is feminine, and therefore should have been *Ka Ktín,* and not *U Ktín,* as an equivalent of ὁ λόγος, although that is masculine in Greek. The French version has *la Parole* (fem.), not *le Parole.* We cannot change the grammar of a language, —Emperors have failed.

§ 114. When identity with the subject is to be asserted, the predicate should take the article.

Nga long *ka* jingshisha, I am THE truth.

Nga long *ka* lynti, I am THE way.

Ka jingim ka la long ka jingshái ki briw, The life was the light of men.

§ 115. Certain nouns in apposition, not intended to mark something specific or individual, but an ordinary title of the person or thing, do not take the Article; as,

U Borsing sím, King Borsing.

U Wat Sirdar, Sirdar Wat.

U Ksan Wadar, Councillor Ksan.

§ 116. All plural nouns, except those used collectively, take the article plural *ki,* and are therefore often used indefinitely; as,

Don *ki briw* ha íng, There are PEOPLE in the house.

La iáp *ki snïang* ha lynti, PIGS died on the road.

La iap-op *ki massi* ha kane ka wah, SOME cows were drowned in this river.

Ki nongôt ki long *ki angel,* The reapers are ANGELS.

§ 117. The article should be repeated in the following cases:—

(1) Before a verb in the *present* tense when it *follows* its nominative; as,

U khlá u ksáw bám ia ki massi, The tiger is continually devouring the cows.

Ka khíh-shoh ka saphrïang, The fever is spreading.

(2) When the verb is in the *future* tense; as,

Ka iew Sohra ka'n long la shái, The Cherra market will be to-morrow.

U kypa u'n phah ktín la shai, His father will send word to-morrow.

(3) Before verbs used negatively; as,

Ka'm treh ka kymi, His mother is not willing.

U lúm u'm da jerong eh, The mountain is not very high.

(4) Before such auxiliary verbs as *da, lah, dang, nang, jiw, &c.*; as,

U Sím u dang lah thaw íng, The king has just built a house.

U khynnah u lah ba'n pule, The lad can read.

U samla u da nang shád bïang eh, The youth can dance very well

Note.—The construction which omits the repeated

article is inelegant, though sometimes heard in ordinary conversation.

The Article and the Objective Case.

§ 118. When the noun in the objective case is governed by the preposition *ia* the article is to be taken definitely; as,

U Siphai u la sïat ia u briw, The Sepoy has shot the man.

Ka huh ka dang kytah ia ka líng, The porpoise has just touched the boat.

§ 119. When the object of the verb is not governed by *ia* the article is often indefinite; as,

U kynda u la pynjot ka íng ha khlàw, The rhinoceros destroyed a house in the jungle.

Ka dingím ka la thàr pathar u snïang, The bear mangled a pig.

§ 120. The article is often omitted before a noun in the objective case.

(1) When it is used indefinitely; as,

U Hat u la leit wád *blang,* Hat is gone in quest of a GOAT.

U Rïang u wan pán *synduk,* Rïang is come to ask for a BOX.

(2) When it is used collectively—

U Lorshái u'n wallam *soh* ia ngi, Lorshái will bring in SOME FRUIT.

Ki nong kitnong, ki kit *briw* mynta, The coolies carry MEN to-day.

§ 121. After prepositions, the article is often omitted, but the noun is definite; as, *Ha íng*, In THE house.

U sim u la hér-noh na *rú*, The bird is flown from THE CAGE.

U snïang u rih hapoh *sem*, The pig is hiding in THE STY.

U iáid-kai halor *lúm*, He is walking on THE MOUNTAIN.

§ 122. The article has sometimes the force of the possessive pronoun; as,

(1) *Ka* kymi ka'm shah ia kata, HIS mother does not allow that.

(2) U Said u dang wád ia *u* khún hangne, Sáid is still searching for HIS son here.

(3) U'm don jaka ba'n buh ia *ka* khlih, He has not where to lay HIS head.

This is identical with a well-known Greek idiom: *οὐκ ἔχει ποῦ τὴν κεφαλὴν κλίνῃ.*—Matt. viii. 20.

§ 123. *The Article before Adjectives not joined to a Substantive.*—The article, when prefixed to an adjective not joined to a substantive, converts it to a noun substantive; as,

ba 'riwbhá, rich; *u ba 'riwbhá*, a rich man.

b'ymman, bad; *u b'ymman*, a bad man.

ki b'ymman, bad men or people; the wicked.

ka 'riwbhá, a rich woman.

§ 124. The feminine article *ka* when so used, forms abstract nouns; as,

ka bymman, evil, wickedness.
ka basníw, badness, wickedness.
ka bahok, justice, righteousness.
ka babhá, goodness.

Note.—For other modes of forming abstracts, see §18, (3).

§ 125. The article is often omitted before nouns connected by *bad*, 'and,' or *bad . . . bad*, 'both . . . and,' whether they be in the nominative or the objective case; as,

(1) *Ki la wan baroh, shinrang bad kynthei*, They all came, male and female.

(2) *Ki la wan, bad shinrang bad kynthei*, They came, both male and female.

(3) *Ki la ioh ia ka spah jong u kypá aroh, bad bri bad khyndew*, They have had all their father's property, both groves and land.

CHAPTER II.

The Noun.

§ 126. *The Nominative.*—When three or more nominatives form the subject to one verb, the conjunctive particle *bad*, 'and,' should only be used between the two last; as,

(1) *Ki ksïar, ki jain, bad ka khyndew, ki'n háp ba-roh ha u khún khadduh,* The gold ornaments, the clothes, and the land will all go to the youngest son.

(2) *U Sím, ki shnong, bad ki dykhàr, ki'n ia sylla lang la shái, nga sngow,* The chief, the villagers, and the Bengalis will hold a consultation to-morrow, I hear.

§ 127. When the verb has several nominatives connected by *bad*, it will require the prefix *ia* to express mutual or joint action; as,

(1) *U Jom bad Ka Bonmai ki la ia rüai ha shnong,* Jom and Bonmai sang in the village.

(2) *U Borsing bad U Ramsing ki la ia sngowthuh,* Borsing and Ramsing have agreed.

§ 128. When a noun is nominative to several verbs, the article should be repeated before each.

(1) *U Said u pang, u khrew, bad u pïaw eh,* Said is ill, weak and very peevish.

(2) *Ka ṁassi ka sngáid, bad ka khráw shisha,* The cow is both fat and big indeed.

(3) *U Sirdar, u beh mrád, u sïat sim, bad u khwái,* The Sirdar hunts, shoots birds, and goes a-fishing.

§ 129. The nominative is as often *expressed* as it is

omitted in the imperative mood, when it should *follow* the verb; as,

(1) Khie leit noh *phi*, Go (YOU) away.

(2) Wat shah ia kata *mé*, Do (THOU) not permit it.

(3) Khymih shane, *phi*, Look here, (YOU).

§ 130. *Number*.—Two or more nominatives connected by *bad*, 'and,' require the article representing them before the verb to be in the plural, that is *ki*, 'they'; as,

(1) Ka shnong bad ka khlấw *ki* iadei ia u sím, The village and the jungle (THEY) belong to the chief.

(2) *U Wadár bad u khun, ki la iáp*, The councillor and his son are dead.

(3) *U nonghikai bad ki khynnah, ki'm put kloi*, The teacher and the children are not yet ready.

§ 131. When the second of two singular nominatives comprehends the first, although connected by *bad*, 'and,' the verb should take the singular article of the second; as,

Ka shnong bad ka muluk baroh, ka la konguh ia u sím, The village and the whole state has submitted to the king.

§ 132. Nominatives of different numbers connected by *bad*, require a plural article before the verb; as,

U ksew bad ki langbrot ki la ngam ryngkat, The dog and the sheep sank together.

§ 133. When the plural nominative is only a secondary

element, the article of the principal nominative only will precede the verb; as,

(1) U nonghikai bad ki khynnah *u* la wan, The teacher with the children HAS come.

(2) U sim bad ki montri, *u* la poi, The chief with his counsellors HAS arrived.

§ 134. When singular nominatives are separated by *lane*, 'or,' *ne*, 'or,' *lymne*, 'nor,' the verb takes the singular article; as,

(1) Ka massi lane ka blang *ka* la pynpráh ia ka jingkér, Either the cow or the goat destroyed the enclosure.

(2) Lymne ka massi, lymne ka blang *ka'm* shym pynprah ia ka jingkér, Neither the cow nor the goat has destroyed the enclosure.

§ 135. When nominatives of different numbers are separated by *lane*, *ne*, or *lymne*, the plural nominative should come last, and the verb will take the plural article; as,

(1) *U kulai lane ki nong kitnong, ki'n kit ia ka mem,* The pony or the coolies will carry the lady.

(2) *U mynthyna lane ki blang ki la khlàw ia ki phán,* Either the gýal or the goats have dug up the potatoes.

§ 136. Collective nouns which convey the idea of unity or oneness take the singular article; as,

Ka muluk baroh *ka* la khih-wìn, THE whole state was disturbed.

U soh *u'm* kynrei ha kane ka snem, The orange is not plentiful this year.

U paitbah *u* wan nguh ia u sím, The people have come to pay their respects to the king.

§ 137. Collective nouns which imply plurality take the plural article; as,

Ki bynriw *ki'm* jiw iamut kajuh, Men never think alike.

Ki paitbah byllin ki la búd ia U Jísu, Great multitudes followed Jesus.

§ 138. *Gender.*—When two or more singular nominatives of different genders are separated by *lane, ne,* or *lymne,* the verb (which should always in this case either precede or immediately follow the first nominative) takes the article and therefore the gender of that first nominative; as,

(1) *Ka'n* iathuh ia phi *ka* kymi, lane u kypá, Either his mother or his father will tell you.

(2) *Ka* ding'ím *kan* bám ia ka blang lane u khlá, Either the bear or the tiger will devour the goat.

Or the verb in this case may remain anarthrous; as,

Yn bám ka dingím lane u khlá ia ka blang.

La tháw u kypá ia ka íng, lane ka kïáw.

The house was built either by his father or his grandmother.

§ 139. Certain collective nouns take both genders, as—

ka muluk=a district, a province, a country. Or,
u muluk=the people who form the community in general.
Ka shnong=lit., a village, a collection of houses; *then* the village in the sense of 'inhabitants'; *or* the village community.
u shnong= the body of the people, the citizens.

Remark.—The feminine form includes all classes, both male and female. The masculine either the male portion, or has an implied reference to the superstitious notion, as in *u shnong*, of a presiding demon, who is thought to dwell mystically *in the people*, and of whose 'voice' and will, the people are an expression in all joint actions.

§ 140. *The Possessive Case.*—The particle *jong* preceding a noun places it in the *Genitive* or *Possessive Case*, as—

Ka íng jong u sim, The chief's house.
Ka kypér jong ki briw, Other people's garden.
Ka mynsím jong nga, My spirit.

§ 141. The particle *jong* (of) is often omitted, as—
Ka-Ktín u Blei, The Word of God.
Ka Mynsím u Blei, The Spirit of God.
Ka íng ki briw, Other people's house.
Ka íng nga, My house.

This mode of expressing possession by mere juxtaposition of nouns should be avoided when it would cause ambiguity ; e.g. *u soh phí* would be inadmissible, as it is also the name of a particular fruit. *Euphony* also (which has great influence on the Khassi language) would often require the form with *jong*.

§ 142. *la* is the Khassi reflexive possessive pronoun always referring back to the subject, as—

U la leit sha la íng, He went to his (own) house.

U Blei U la ái ia la U Khún, God gave His (own) Son.

Remark.—Those acquainted with Bengali, &c., will see that this particle *la* in Khassi is equivalent to the Bengali আপন, and the Hindustani اپنا (*ápná*). See § 56.

§ 143. Various prepositions and phrases often require the possessive with *jong* after them, as, *shaphang*, 'concerning,' *nalor*, 'besides,' *hamar*, 'about,' *namar*, 'on account of,' *na ka bynta*, 'for the sake,' &c.

U kren shaphang jong phi, He speaks of you.

Nalor jong phi ym don shuh, Beside you there is no one.

U sngowsih namar jong nga, He is vexed on my account.

U la iáp na ka bynta jong ngi, He died for our sake.

§ 144. *The Objective Case.*—Nouns and their substitutes in the objective case generally take *ia* before them after transitive verbs, as—

U khlá u kem niat *ia* ka miáw, The tiger seized the cat.

U kobiraj u la pynjem *ia* ka jingpang, The doctor has eased the pain.

See §§ 118, 119, 120.

§ 145. The objective particle *ia* is never used before anarthrous nouns; hence it is often dispensed with in the objective case, as—

U Míet u pyniap *massi*, Miet kills beef.

U Ronsing u shoh *briw*, Ronsing is beating people.

§ 146. When objectives are *anarthrous* they are used indefinitely, and are generally plural—

U Sím u'n ái *briw* mynta, The chief will give men to-day.

Ka tymen ka kit *sïar*, The old woman carries fowls.

See § 118.

§ 147. When the objective case *precedes* the verb, the sentence is then emphatic—

Ia ka massi u la pyniap, He HAS killed the cow.

Ia ka tyngka u la shem, He HAS found the money.

§ 148. In many instances the objective has become, as it were, a part of the verb, such as—

khwái-doh-khá, to fish, lit. to hook fish.

tong-úm, to draw water.

tong-shér, to catch small fish or sprats.

rïam-sim, to catch (birds).

kheit-soh, to gather (fruit).

thoh-díng, to cut wood.

pynmih-snám, to bleed, lit. to cause blood to come out.

§ 149. Some verbs are followed by two objectives, one being a more exact definition of the other, and without the article. It is *the accusative of closer definition* of classic authors, as—

U Hakim u la kynnoh *nongtuh* ia ngạ, The judge accused me (of being) A THIEF=The judge called me A THIEF.

U Shnong u'n sa thung *sím* ia u syrdar, The village will appoint the sirdar KING.

U Blei u pynlong *'ríw-khúid* ia ki bangeit, God makes SAINTS of believers.

Remark.—Closely allied to these are those accusatives which often follow certain adjectives, as—

U nonghikai u khraw *ka jingstád,* The teacher is eminent (for his) learning.

U long u ba da heh noh *ka rynieng,* He is very big as to his stature.

§ 150. *Cognate Accusatives* are somewhat numerous in Khassi, but difficult to translate literally.

phah-jingphah, to send something (that should be sent).

wád-jingwád, to search for something.

kit-jingkit, to carry burdens.

wan-jingwan, to return from a journey.

leit-jingleit, to go on a journey.

thíed-jingthíed, to buy goods.

die-jingdie, to sell goods.

dih-jingdih, to drink something.
bám-jingbám, to eat something.

These accusatives are all used in a very general and indefinite sense.

§ 151. The objective may be a sentence introduced by *ba* (that), or a verb in the infinitive mood, as—

(1) *U Sím u la adong ba'n iám-briw la shái*, The chief has forbidden to mourn to-morrow.

(2) *Nga tip ba phi ïeit ia nga*, I know that you love me.

Ki ong ba ka la ing ka íng, They say that the house went on fire.

§ 152. *The Dative.*—This case often represents the remoter object of certain verbs, and is preceded by the particles *ia* and *ha*, 'to,' 'for'; an application of *ia* different from that explained already.

(1) Nga la ái ia ka kitab *ia* u saheb, I gave the book TO the gentleman.

(2) Nga la ai ia ka kitab *ha* phi, I gave the book TO you.

(3) U khynnah u pán kháw *ia* u kypa, The lad is begging rice FOR his father.

(4) Ka massi ka bat ka dud *ia* la u khún, The cow withholds her milk FOR her calf.

Note.—*Ia* denotes the object 'for which,' or the person 'to,' or *for whose sake*, anything is done or given; *ha* merely implies that something has been done 'to,' i.e. in the presence, or in the hearing, but not in the interest of that person. Example 2 simply means that the book was left with, and not given for a possession.

§ 153. *The Instrumental Case.* — 1. The instrument used in performing any action is distinguished by the particle *da* (by, with, through). 2. The material with or out of which anything is prepared is also indicated by *da* (with, of).

(1) Ngi jiw pyniap snïang *da* ka tari, We kill pigs with a knife.

Ki Khassi ki jiw pyniap snïang *da* u speh, The Khassis kill pigs WITH a pointed bamboo.

La pynrem ia u briw *da* ka jingbishár ba hok, The man was condemned BY just trial.

La pyllait ia phi *da* ka jing ia sait jong nga, You were released THROUGH my intercession.

(2) U Rïang u tháw la ka ing *da* ka surkhi, Rïang builds his house WITH mortar.

U Rïang u tháw la ka kynroh *da* u máw, Rïang builds his wall OF stone.

§ 154. *The Locative.*—The idea of location or position is expressed by the preposition *ha* (in), and sometimes by *sha*, though the primary meaning of the latter is 'to,' with verbs of motion.

Ka kitab ka don *ha* nga, The book is WITH me.

U kulai u thïah *ha* sem, The horse is lying IN the stable.

U Trái u'm put don *ha* íng, The master is not yet at home.

U'm put don *sha* u,* He is not yet at home.

Ki blang jong nga ki iabám kynbat *sha* khláw, My goats are eating medicinal herbs IN the jungle.

CHAPTER III.

The Adjective.

§ 155. For the position of the adjective and article, read again the sections in the etymological part of this Grammar, and §§ 96, 97 of the Syntax.

§ 156. When the adjective precedes (*sic*) its noun, it is predicative, and not a mere attribute. The verb 'to be' (*long*) is understood, see § 97; as—

(1) *U babhá u briw,* is not, A good man, but lit. Good (is) the man=The man (is) good.

(2) *Ka bashisha ka ktín U Blei,* is not, The true Word of God, but, True (is) the Word of God=The Word of God (is) true.

§ 157. Care should be taken not to confound the

* The French *chez lui*, 'at home,'

particle *ba* as an adjective prefix, with the conjunction *ba* (that, or because) when it precedes an adjective at the beginning of a sentence or clause. In that case *ba* is a conjunction, or a causal particle signifying 'because,' introducing an elliptical phrase, and should stand quite separate from the adjective; as—

Ba sníw ki dohkhá, not *Basníw ki doh khá*, Because the fish (are) bad.

The clause in full would stand thus:—

Ba ki long sníw ki dohkhá, Because the fish are bad.

U'm ïeit ia u nonghikai, *ba íhsih u briw*, He loves not the master, BECAUSE THE MAN (IS) HATEFUL.

U'm shym thíed, *ba lamwir u ksew*, He did not buy, BECAUSE THE DOG (was) MAD.

U'm lah kíw, *ba jerong eh u lúm*, He was not able to ascend, BECAUSE THE MOUNTAIN (is) TOO HIGH.

§ 158. Besides the cases mentioned under § 35, the prefix *ba* is omitted also when the adjective is predicative with or without the verb expressed; as—

U khynnah u tipsngi eh, The lad is very wise.

U ksew u lamwir, The dog is mad.

U phan u khyndiat, The potato is scarce.

In this construction the adjective without *ba* must always take the article of the noun it qualifies.

§ 159. An adjective qualifying two or more nouns connected by *bad* (and) takes the plural article—

U kypá bad u khún ki long *ki* baíhbhá, The father and his son are handsome.

U massi-dáb bad ka blang *ki* sngáid shisha, The ox and the goat are fat indeed.

§ 160. When the verb is expressed, the position of the adjective will vary according to the emphasis—

(1) *U briw u long u bastád*, The man is wise.
U long u bastád u briw, He is a wise man.
U bastád u long u briw, Wise is the man.

(2) *Ka sïar ka long ka basngáid*, The hen is fat.
Ka long ka basngáid ka sïar, It is a fat hen.
Ka basngáid ka long ka sïar, Fat is the hen.

§ 161. When nouns of different genders are separated by *lane* (or), the adjective should take the article of the first, and either precede or immediately follow it; as—

Ka shakri *ka balah* ba'n leit, lane u khynnah, The servant girl or the lad can go.

U soh *n jew* lane ka dud, The fruit or the milk is sour.

Should the adjective follow the last noun, it will not take the article accordingly.

Ka shakri lane u khynnah balah ba'n leit, It is the servant girl or the lad that is able to go.

§ 162. *Numerals.*—With numeral adjectives *ngut* is used in the case of persons, and *tylli* in that of animals and inanimate objects—

Don ar *tylli* ki sim ha rú, There are two birds in the cage.

Lái tylli ki mrâd ki la ia mih na khláw, Three animals came out of the jungle.

Ngi la ioh íh *lái ngut* ki kynthei hangta, We saw three women there.

Don *lai ngut* ki sím hapoh shnong, There are three chiefs in the village.

§ 163. We here give examples of the arrangement and use of the adjectives of indefinite quantity: *baroh*, 'all;' *baroh phar*, 'entirely;' *baroh phit*, 'entirely;' *bún*, 'much;' *shibún*, 'much,' 'many.'

(1)	Ka íng *baroh*, ka la ing. Ka íng, ka la ing *baroh*.	The whole house was burnt.
(2)	Ki la pang ha íng *baroh*. Ki la pang *baroh* ha íng.	They were all ill at home.
(3)	Ka pyrthei *baroh phar* ka sníw. Ka pyrthei ka sníw *baroh phar*.	The world is corrupt all over.
(4)	Ki briw *bún* ki la iáp. Ki la iáp *bún* briw.	Many people died.
(5)	*Ka spah bún ka la duh.* *Ka la duh bún spah.*	Much wealth was lost.

(6) *Ka spah shibún ka mih nangta*, Much wealth comes from there.

(7) *Ki briw shibún ki iapom*, Many people are fighting.

The Degrees of Comparison.

§ 164. *Equality* and *Similarity* are expressed by the particles *kat*, *kumba*, *kum*, *shi*, and by the correlatives *shi. . . . bad*, *kajuh. . . . bad.*

(1) U jerong *kat* phi, He is AS tall AS you (are).
Lit.—He is tall, LIKE you, *or*, He is tall, AS you are.

(2) U long 'riwbhá *kum* phi, He is AS rich AS you.

(3) Kane ka kypér ka mih soh *kum* ka jong nga, This garden is AS productive AS mine.
Lit.—This garden is productive AS mine (is).

(4) Kane ka kypér ka mih soh *kajuh kum* ka jong nga, This garden is AS productive AS my own.

(5) Ki khynnah kine ki ialong baroh *shi* rynieng, These children are all OF THE SAME stature.

(6) U saheb u long *shi* jingmut *bad* nga hí, The gentleman is of the SAME opinion AS myself.

(7) U syrdar u don kajuh ka bor bad nga hí, The sirdar has the SAME authority AS myself.

§ 165. *Kham. . . . ia* (more. . . . than), are used to express the possession of a quality in a higher or lower degree; as—

(1) U sohiong u *kham* thïang *ia* u soh kait, The black plum is sweeter THAN the citron.

(2) U soh phíng u *kham* kynrei *ia* u soh poh hangne, The mangoe is MORE plentiful here THAN the apple.

§ 166. Sometimes the particle *kham* (more) may be

dispensed with, the simple positive with *ia* being sufficient, but the order of the words is changed; as—

(1) *Ia* u soh poh, thïang u sohmon, The pear is sweeter than the apple.

(2) *Ia* ka ba'n sníw, *bhá* ba'n iáp, It is BETTER to die THAN to be wicked.

§ 167. *Kham* is often used to express a quality in its highest degree, without any comparison implied with any other specified object; as—

Une u briw u *kham* rúnar shisha, This man is VERY cruel indeed.

Ka shnong ka la kham kyrduh shisha, The village has become VERY poor indeed.

In this construction *kham* may often have the sense of our 'rather,' as—

U *kham* íh shisha une u soh, This fruit is indeed rather ripe.

U kham bhá une u briw, He is rather a good fellow.

§ 168. The following forms should be mastered :—

(1) U briw u sníw *khyndiat,* The man is RATHER bad.

(2) *U briw u kham sníw khyndiat,* The man is rather worse.

(3) *U briw u kham sníw pat,* The man is still worse.

(4) *U briw u kham sníw pynban,* The man is yet worse.

(5) *U briw u kham sníw shibún,* The man is much worse.

(6) *U briw u'm kham sníw shuh,* The man is no worse.

(7) *U briw u kham bhá shibún,* The man is much better.

(8) *U briw u'm kham bhá shibún,* The man is not much better.

§ 169. From the examples given of comparison between two objects, it will be seen that our 'than' is represented by *ia* in Khassi; as—

(1) Une u khynnah u kham bhá *ia* la u kypá, This lad is better THAN his father.

(2) *U Tirot u la long kham shlur ia ki sím Khassi baroh,* Tirot was more courageous than all the Khassi chiefs.

§ 170. The ordinary SUPERLATIVE, or the SUPERLATIVE RELATIVE, as some would call it, is expressed in two ways, *either* by the simple positive, or the comparative with a noun in an oblique case governed by *na*—the Bengali হইতে and Hindústani سے. Or by the simple positive or the comparative with the prepositional phrase *ha pyddeng,* the *Bengali* মধ্যে and *Hindústani* کا بیچ میں (*ka bich men*); as—

(1) Na kine ki máw *rit* une (positive), This is the smallest of these stones.

Na kine ki máw, *kham rit* une, (comparative), This is the smallest of these stones.

Na kine ki lynti, *jing-ngái* ka lynti Shillong (positive), Of these routes, the furthest is the Shillong route.

Na kine ki lynti, kham jing-ngai ka lynti Shillong, (comparative), Of these routes, the furthest is the Shillong route.

Remark.—This evidently corresponds with the *Bengali* and *Hindústani* idiom, with the ablative হইতে and سے respectively; thus, তাহাহইতে সেই ভাল, یہ اُس سے اچّھا ہي

(2) Ha pyddeng ki mrád *baroh shlúr* u sing (positive).
Ha pyddeng ki mrád *kham shlúr* u sing (comparative), Of all the beasts, the lion is the MOST courageous.

Remark.—This construction with *ha pyddeng* (among) corresponds with the Bengali idiom, তাহাদের মধ্যে তুমি ভাল *Táhádér madhye tumi bhalo,* You are the best of them.

§ 171. The particle *ia* is also used in the superlative construction for our 'of' as well as 'than;' as—

Ia kine baroh bhá maphi, You are the best OF them all, *or,* You are better THAN all these.

§ 172. The SUPERLATIVE ABSOLUTE—that is, the *highest* or *lowest* degree of any quality—is expressed in various ways, by the addition of any of the following words or phrases: *tam, eh, shik-kadei, kham tam, tam eh.*

Ka já ka long ka jingbám ka ba bhá tam, Boiled rice is the best food.

Ka shini ka long ka jingdie kaba thïang tam, Sugar is the sweetest commodity.

Ki niéw ka sherita ka jhúr ka bakthang tam eh, They consider wormwood the most bitter of herbs.

Une U lúm u da jerong shikkadei eh, This mountain is exceedingly high.

Nga tip ba phi long u bakham rúnar tam ba nga la iòh íh, I know that you are the most cruel man I have seen.

Remarks.—Tam has in Khassi often the force of an independent verb, and signifies 'to exceed;' as—

U Rising u la tam ia ngi baroh, Rising has gone beyond us all.

U Sím u la tam ia la ka bor, The chief has exceeded his power.

Kane ka díng ka tam shi pruh, This stick exceeds *or* is over one cubit.

This particle *tam* is probably the Bengali suffix তম (*tam*). While it is very probable that in an earlier stage of the (Bengali) language it was used as an independent word, though now reduced to a mere suffix, it is interesting to note that in Khassi it still retains more or less its original force both as a particle of comparison and as an independent verb.

Tam sometimes signifies 'too much,' as the French *trop;* as—

U khynnah u la kren *tam,* The lad spoke TOO MUCH.

Tam sometimes signifies 'more'; as—

Phi da sngowbhá ba'n ái *tam* ia kaba u la ong? Will you kindly give MORE than he ordered?

CHAPTER IV.

The Pronouns.

§ 173. When the articles *u, ka* and *ki* are used alone in a sentence, they are strictly Personal Pronouns; as—

U la hïar sha thor mynhynne, HE went down to the plains this morning.

Ki la ia wan-ruing bad u phan, THEY returned the same day with potatoes.

Remark.—The article was *originally* a Demonstrative Pronoun, of which character the Personal Pronouns of the third person still often partake.

§ 173. The article thus employed must agree in number and gender with the noun it represents in a sentence.

U nonghikai jong ngi, *u* hikai bhá eh, Our teacher teaches very well.

Ka íng-massi *ka* la pluh noh, The cowhouse (IT) is burnt down.

§ 174. Two or more nominatives, though of different

genders, connected by *bad* (and) require the pronoun to be in the plural; as,

U Saheb bad ka mem *ki* long Phareng,* The gentleman and his wife (THEY) are English.

U ksew bad ka miáw, *ki* iadat, The dog and the cat (THEY) are fighting.

§ 175. When these nominatives are personal pronouns, one of which is in the *first person*, the personal pronoun which will represent them as the direct nominative (*in apposition*) of the verb, should be in the *first person plural;* as,

(1.) Ma-nga bad ma-phi, *ngi'n* ia leit-kái sha shnong, I and you, (WE) will go on a visit to the village.

(2.) Ma-u bad ma-nga, *ngi'n* ia leit noh ryngkat, He and I, (WE) will go away together.

(3.) *Ngi'n* ia iáp lem, ma-nga bad ma-ki, Both I and they, (WE) will die together.

§ 176. When the personal pronouns thus connected by *bad* are of the *second* and *third* person, singular or plural, the pronoun which represents them should be in the *second person plural;* as,

Ma-u bad ma-phi, *phi'n* ioh shitom, *Or*, *Phi'n* ioh shitom, ma-u bad ma-phi, You will come to trouble, both he and you. *Phi'n* jot noh thïáw, ma-mé bad ma-ki, You will be utterly ruined, both you and they.

* A corruption of 'Feringhi,' lit., *Frenchmen*, the first known to the natives, from ফিরিং

§ 177. The pronomial article is *omitted* before a verb in the past tense after personal pronouns separated by *lane, ne,* 'or' *lymne,* 'nor,' unless the verb comes between these nominatives, which is often the order followed; as,

Manga lane ma-phi la ong ia kata, Either I or you said so.

Or, *La ong ia kata ma-ngà, lane ma-phi,*

Or, *Nga la ong ia kata manga, lane ma-phi.*

Ym shym ong ia kata, lymne ma-nga lymne ma-phi, Neither you nor I said so.

The same rule applies when the verb is in the *future tense;* as,

Yn ioh bainong ma-u lane ma-phi, Either he or you will have wages.

Or, *Ma-u, u'n ioh bainong, lane ma-phi,*

U'n ym ioh bainong, lymne ma-u lymne ma-phi,

Neither he nor you will have wages.

§ 178. When the verb is in the *present tense,* the nominatives separated by *lane* should not follow in immediate succession, or, the verb should precede the pronouns, with the first pronoun for its direct nominative.

(1.) *Ma-u u pang lane ma-phi,* or,

(2.) *U pang ma-u, lane ma-phi,* Either he or you are ill.

(1.) *Ma-nga nga shitom, lane ma-phi,* or,

(2.) *Nga shitom manga lane ma-phi,* Either I or you are in trouble.

§ 179. The form of the personal pronoun with *ma-* are in the majority of cases used (1) *disjunctively* like the French *moi, toi, lui,* &c., to add emphasis; (2) *honorifically,* but (3) in a few instances *euphonically;* as,

(1.) Nga la ong, *ma-nga.* I said. Je-dis, MOI.
(2.) Me la wan, *ma-mé.* THOU hast come. Tu est venu, TOI.
(3.) U la kren, *ma-u.* He spoke. C'est LUI, qui a parlé.
(4.) Tó wan *ma-phi.* Come, *or* YOU come. Viens, TOI.
(5.) Phi'n wan *ma-phi?* Will YOU come? Viendrez vous?

Remark.—In all the above, the pronouns with *ma-* cannot be the direct nominative, except with verbs of command, and the future with *yn.* Nor is it our emphatic form with 'self,' as some have alleged, for—

§ 180. The true emphatic personal pronoun corresponding to our English 'self,' the Latin 'ipse,' or French 'même,' is always formed in Khassi with *hí,* 'self'; as,

(1.) U Sím u la ong *hí,* The king said HIMSELF, *or,*
U Sím *hí* u la ong, The king HIMSELF said, *or,*
U la ong *hí* u Sim, The king said HIMSELF.

(2.) U Sím u la ong *ma-u hí*
U Sím *ma-u hí* u la ong.
U la ong *ma-u hí* u Sím.
} The king said HIMSELF. Note here that *ma-u* is used *honorifically.*

Phi'n ong hí ma-phi? Will you say yourself?

In the same way *hí* may be used when the nominative is a personal pronoun, and *ma-u, &c.*, may be added *honorifically*, or for the sake of *euphony*

U la ong hí.
U la ong hí ma-u. } He HIMSELF said.
U la ong ma-u hí.

The student would do well to write out these forms with other verbs such as *wan*, 'to come,' *kren*, 'to speak,' *sngow*, 'to hear.'

§ 181. The much disputed idiom 'It is me' in English should be rendered as follows in Khassi:

Ka long ma-nga, It is me. French, *C'est moi.*
Ka long ma-phi, It is you. „ *C'est vous.*
Ka long ma-u, It is him. „ *C'est lui.*

Remarks.—*hí* and *ma-u hí, ma-ka hí*, &c., are analogous to and even identical with আপনি and اپ (*áp*) in Bengali and Hindústani.

আমি আপনি উত্তর দিলাম I myself answered.
مین اپ بولا I myself said.

§ 182. *The Possessive Pronoun.*—The usual particle of possession *jong* is often omitted in certain set phrases, as *Ka íng nga, Ka íng phi, Ka íng u*, for *Kà íng jong nga, &c.* My house, Your house, &c. But the rule is to employ *jong* before personal pronouns.

Ka wait jong phi ka la lúin eh, Your cleaver (*dáw*) is very blunt.

Ka íng jong u ka sa noh sha rïat, His house will fall over the precipice presently.

The omission of *jong* before nouns is both regular and elegant. (See § 141.)

§ 183. The article has sometimes the force of a possessive pronoun. (See § 122.)

U saheb u la khein *ka kyjat,* The gentleman has broken HIS leg.

Phi la khein *ka* byniat, You have broken YOUR tooth.

§ 184. When the article separates the possessive from the object possessed, then the clause is an assertion ; as,

Ka íng, *ka* jong nga, The house (is) MINE.

Ka jong nga, *ka* íng, MINE (is) the house.

The prefix *jing* of abstract nouns is only another form of this *jong,* 'of.'

§ 185. *The reflexives la, la ka jong, la u jong, la hí, la ka jong hí, la u jong hí,* which all mean, 'his,' 'her,' 'its,' &c., 'his own,' 'her own,' 'its own,' &c., refer to the nominative of the principal verb, and differ essentially from the construction with *jong.* When *hí* is added to *la, la ka, la u, la ka jong, &c.,* it is equivalent to our word 'own' in English and to আপন, اپنا (*ápan, ápná*) in Bengali and Hindústani, and the Latin suus, sua, suum ; as,

U la die-noh *la* ka íng, He sold HIS house.

Ka la thei la ka íng, She has built HER house.

Ka kymi jong phi ka pynjot ia *la* ka íng *hí*, Your mother is ruining HER OWN family.

Nga la khein ia *la* ka kyjat, I have broken MY leg.

Nga la khein ia la ka jang ka kyjat, I have broken my own leg.

Remark.—If *jong* had been used here, the possessive would refer to some person other than that represented by the *nominative.*

§ 186. The absolute possessives, 'mine,' 'thine,' 'his,' 'her,' 'yours,' 'ours,' &c., formed by prefixing the proper article of the thing possessed before the ordinary possessive case of the personal pronoun, is a very common construction in Khassi; as,

Kane ka long *ka jong nga*, This is MINE.

Kane ka dei *ka jong nga*, This is MINE, *or*, belongs to me.

Shaphang kata ka íng, ka long *ka jong phi*, As to that house, it is yours.

Ka kyper ka'm jiw la dei *ka jong phi*, The garden was never YOURS.

§ 187. The reflexive 'self' is also rendered in Khassi by *lade* or *lade hí.*

U la shukor ia *lade*, He deceived HIMSELF.

Ka la khein duh ia *lade*, She gave HERSELF up for lost.

Phi la rïam bïeit ia *lade*, You have foolishly entangled YOURSELF.

(1.) Prepositional clauses are made reflexive by means of *la:*

U la phet da *la* ka món hí, He went away of his own accord.

U la leit noh sha *la* ka íng, He went away to HIS OWN home.

(2.) Sometimes, as in English, this construction may be ambiguous; as,

U Daroga u la kem ia u briw ha *la* íng hí, The Inspector arrested the man in HIS OWN house.

Tó âi noh ia nga *la* ka jong, Give me MY OWN. Might =Give me YOUR own.

(3.) When the verb is transitive, the emphatic *hí*, 'self,' when it refers to the subject should follow the latter or the verb, and the object when it refers to it.

U Sím *hí*, u la pyniap ia u nongtuh, The chief himself killed the thief.

U Sím u la pyniap ia u nongtuh *hí*, The chief killed the VERY thief.

§ 188. *The Relative Pronoun.*—The true relative pronoun in Khassi is the conjunctive particle *ba*, originally signifying *that, because, since.* The forms *uba, kaba, kiba,* commonly called relatives, are in reality both antecedent and relative, for (1) *ba* is often and elegantly used alone; (2) the compound forms *kaba, uba,* &c., may also be the subject of a principal sentence.

(1.) Nga íhthúh ia u briw *ba* phi la mudui, I know the man WHOM you have sued.

The Relative here is evidently *ba*.

(2.) *Kaba* la jïa sha shnong, ka mih na ka jingshún, WHAT happened in the village, arises from enmity.

From this example it is evident that *kaba* contains the antecedent *ka* and the relative *ba*. So that *uba, kaba,* &c., in all cases mean 'that which,' 'he who,' &c. Another proof that the article was originally a *demonstrative.*

§ 189. The article prefixed to *ba* in the formation of the relative in many sentences is only the article repeated according to the rule already explained; as,

Ka samla, *kaba* wan mynhynnin, ka la iáp, The girl THAT came yesterday is dead.

§ 190. The relative generally follows immediately its antecedent; as,

Ka lyngkhá, *ba* nga la bet, ka sei soh bïang, The field which I sowed, bears fruit well.

U lúm, *uba* páw hangta, u jerong eh, The mountain WHICH appears there is very high.

Caution.—Care, however, should be taken not to confound the relative *ba* with the conjunction *ba,* though originally identical.

(1.) Nga tip *ba* phi la leh ia kata, I know THAT you have done that.

(2.) Nga íhthuh ia phi, *ba* la leh ia kata, I know you who have done that.

§ 191. When the relative is in the accusative case, it often takes *ia* before it; as,

(1.) Nga sngowthuh bhá *ia kaba* phi ong, I understand well WHAT you say.

(2.) *Nga wan thang ia u briw, ia uba la pyniap*, &c., I have been burning the man WHO was killed, &c.

Remark 1.—The Khassi language being devoid of inflection, in the strict sense of that word, it cannot have what Greek grammarians call *attraction.* We have, however, several instances in the version of the New Testament, of this peculiarity of Greek grammar being introduced.

When the relative in the original, though itself the subject of its own verb, agrees, for example, in the accusative case with its antecedent, or is in the genitive by attraction, the relative in Khassi, in order to preserve a literal (?) rendering, is put in the same case; but contrary to usage. John v. 23, is a case in point; and when rendered into English would translate "*whom* hath sent him." The verse should be rendered thus:—

U'm burom ia u kypá *uba* la phah ia u, He honoureth not the Father which hath sent him.

Remark 2.—To use the so-called relatives *u-ba, ka-ba, ki-ba,* which signify 'he who,' 'she who,' &c., as substitutes for the Greek article is unwarrantable both by grammar and practice.

§ 192. THE DEMONSTRATIVE PRONOUNS.—The article has often the force of a demonstrative ; as,

U briw u la lah poi, THE man has arrived.

Nga'm ioh íh ia *ka* íng, I do not see THE house.

§ 193. The demonstratives are formed from the simple article by the addition of suffixes to denote nearness or remoteness ; as, *ka-ne, u-ne, ki-ne,* in which *-ne* denotes 'here' (this, these) ; *ka-ta, u-ta, ki-ta,* where *-ta* denotes 'there' entirely out of sight; but *-to, -tai,* different degrees of distance, to *within* sight, as *kito, kitai.* (See § 53.)

§ 194. The demonstratives, like nouns, always require the article to follow them in a sentence :

(1.) *Uto u kulai u la dykhoh,* That horse is lame.

(2.) *Ine i sïar i la sydang khá-pylleng,* This chicken has commenced laying eggs.

(3.) Lehse *kita,* kiba poi mynsngi, ki-tip baroh, Perhaps those who arrived at mid-day, know all.

(4.) Nga'm sngowthuh ia *kine ki ktín* jong phi, I do not understand THESE WORDS of yours.

§ 195. *The Distributives.*—We shall here merely give

examples of their use. For mode of their formation, see § 54.

(1.) *Uwei-uwei* u'n ioh la ka bainong, EACH will have his wages.

Nga'n pyllait ia ki kynthei *kawei-kawei*, I will let go the women, ONE BY ONE.

(2.) Distribution is expressed by *mar*, 'each.'

Ki nongtrei ki'n ioh mar-shi tyngka, The workmen will have one rupee each.

Ki nongtrei ki la ioh mar shi tyngka-tyngka, The workmen received one rupee each.

Ki la búd ia ka met iáp mar arngut-arngut, They followed the corpse two-by-two.

(3.) By the insertion of *-pa-*.

Ngi'n ia búd ia -phi *uwei-pa-uwei*, (masc.), We will follow you ONE-BY-ONE.

Ki kynthei ki la iakren *kawei-pa-kawei*, (fem.), The women spoke ONE-BY-ONE.

Ki la ia kylli ia ki uwei-pa-kawei, (masc. and fem.), They asked them ONE-BY-ONE, (both male and female.)

(4.) *ruh* (also) appended.

Uwei-uwei-ruh u'n ioh ia kren bad nga, EACH ONE will be allowed to speak with me.

Ki'n die ia ki íng *kawei-kawei-ruh* kyrphang, They will sell the houses ONE BY ONE, separately

(5.) Another mode with *na—sha.*

Ki la ia wád ia 'u briw *na kawei-sha kawei* pat ka íng, They searched for the man FROM ONE house TO ANOTHER.

(6.) "Either" is expressed by *uwei na*, lit.=' one of' (masc.), '*kawei na*' (fem.), and 'neither' by these followed by a negative (*'m*).

U Saheb u'n ái kam ia *uwei na* kine ki samla, The gentleman will give employment to EITHER of these youths.

Uwei ruh *na* kine, u'n ym sngowbhá ba'n leit, NEITHER of these will like to go.

Remark.—It will be seen from the above that the idea of individual distribution is conveyed by reduplication of either noun or pronoun, with or without *mar* (each).

Ki siphai ki la ia bysut *arngut-arngut*, The soldiers entered TWO-BY-TWO.

Ngi'n ia ái jubáb *marwei-marwei*, We will reply INDIVIDUALLY, OR ONE-BY-ONE.

Ngi'n ia tháw la *ka íng–ka íng*, We will build EVERY ONE his own house.

Ngi'n ia trei ha la *ka kam–ka kam*, We will work EACH at his own occupation.

§ 196. Our 'each' is also expressed in Khassi by the indef. pronoun *uwei* or *kawei*, or *iwei*.

Ki kynthei ki'n ioh ár tyngka *kawei*, The women will receive two rupees EACH.

§ 197. *The Indefinite Pronouns*, for a list of which see under § 55, may be illustrated by the following examples:—

Ki la sngowsih eh *baroh* ha ĭng, They were ALL very much displeased at home.

Ki khynnah ki la sngow bukhoh eh *baroh ár*, The lads were BOTH very much disappointed.

La ĭng ka íng *baroh kawei*, The WHOLE house was burnt.

U la win u lúm *baroh uwei*, The WHOLE mountain shook.

Uwei-pat u'n bujli ia u, ANOTHER will take his place.

Uno-uno-ruh u da lah ba'n leh ia kata, ANY ONE could do that.

Uno-ruh-uno u lah ba'n leh ia kata, SOMEBODY OR ANOTHER may do that.

Kino-kino-ruh ki'n ià wan wád iá u ksew, SOME (persons) will come after the dog.

Kino-ruh-kino ki'n ia wan wád ia u ksew, SOME PERSONS OR OTHER will come after the dog.

La poi shane *wei-ruh-wei* mynhynne mynstep, SOMEBODY OR ANOTHER came here this morning.

La jïa *ei-ruh-ei*, nga'm tip shuh, Something has happened, I don't know at all what.

Uwei u la kren, te *uwei pat* u la batai, One spoke, and the other explained.

Ki ba'n wád ia u ksew ruh don kein, SOME (people) will come after the dog also of course.

Tang *khyndiat* ki wan ia seng mynta, Only a FEW came to the meeting to-day.

Bún ki la wan ia seng mynhynnin, Many came to the meeting yesterday.

Nga'm don soh, tó ái *katto-katne* hó, I have no oranges, do give me some, will you?

Ei-ei-ruh-em nga'*m* lah ong shuh, I can say NOTHING at all.

Ei-ei-ruh-ém ym don ha íng, There is nothing in the house.

Contrary to other languages, we have in the two last examples, two negatives used to express a negation.

§ 198. *The Interrogative Pronouns* are underlined in the following examples.

Ei ba kren? Who speaks?

Ei ba iathuh? Who said?

Uei ba'n leit wád briw? Who will go for coolies?

Mano? WHO is there?

Kaei phi ong? What do you say?

Kiei ba'n kit jongkit? Who are (to be) the coolies?

Aiuh phi kren? *or*, Phi kren *aiuh?* What do you say?

Phi kren shaphang *aiuh?* What are you talking about?

Yn kren U Sím. *Uno?* The king will speak. WHO?

Tó shim ia kane. *Kano?* Take this, will you. WHICH?

Kane ka *jong no?* Whose is this?

Iano phi la ia kren baroh shi katta? OF WHOM were you speaking all that while?

Hano phi la ái ia kata ka kitab? To WHOM did you give that book?

Nang-no phi la ioh ia kane ka ing? From *or* Of whom did you get this house?

Nga'n leit lah shemphang *aiuh* ia kata baroh? WHAT can I know of all that business?

Da-ei phi'n tháw ia la ka íng? WITH *or* OF WHAT will you build your house?

Kum kaei long kata ka líng-tydem? WHAT SORT (of a thing) is that steamboat? (See § 215.)

§ 199. *The Compound Relatives.*—We shall give here a few examples, merely to illustrate the list given under § 52.

Uno-uno-ruh uba ngeit, u'n ioh jingim, WHOSOEVER believeth will have life.

Jar uba ngeit u'n ioh jingim b'ym jiw-kut, WHOSOEVER believeth will have life eternal.

Ia u kulai, la' *u* long *u jongno-jongno ruh,* yn die noh, The horse, WHOSE-SOEVER it is, will be sold.

Uno-uno-ruh, uba ka dohnúd jong u ka sníw, yn long sníw ka kam jong u ruh, WHOEVER has a bad heart, will also have bad actions.

Ha uno-uno-ruh ba phi shanïa, ia uta phi'n ieit kein;

Uno-uno-ruh ha uba phi shanïa, ia uta phi'n ïeit kein, IN WHOMSOEVER you trust, him you will love of course.

Ia kaei-kaei-ruh ba mé leh, to leh katba mé lah, WHATEVER thou doest, do with all thy might.

Jaid ba kylla jingmut shibún, ym lah shanïa ha u, WHOEVER changes his mind often, (he) cannot be trusted.

Note.—From the above examples it will be observed that the *compound relative* is formed by combining the *indefinite pronouns* with the simple relative *ba*, or with *uba*, *kaba*, &c.

CHAPTER V.

The Verb.

§ 200. The verb 'to be,' or *long*, is often omitted or understood in Khassi; as—

U lúm Rab-leng u'm da jerong eh, Rableng mountain (IS) not very high.

Ka sngi ka kham khráw shibún ia U Bynái, The sun (IS) much larger than the moon.

U khynnah u tipsngi eh naduh ba u shong skúr, The lad (IS) very well behaved since he is at school.

Note.—This feature might perhaps be explained by maintaining that the *adjectives* as well as the *adverbs* become in monosyllabic languages virtually verbs by *construction.*

§ 201. *Voice.* — Some verbs, originally *intransitive,* are often used *transitively,* but with a change of meaning; as,

(1.) *Mih*=' to rise,' ' to spring,' or ' to accrue.' (Intransitive).

U phlang u la *mih* kloi eh ha kane ka snem, The grass has SPRUNG up very early this spring.

Ka sngi ka *mih* ha mih-'ngi, The sun RISES in the east.

Mih (transitive)=' to produce,' ' to yield.'

Kane ka lyngkhá ka *mih* phan shibún, This field YIELDS a good crop of potatoes.

Une u lúm u *mih* dewiong shikkadei, This hill YIELDS a great deal of coal.

(2.) *Ïeng* (intransitive)=' to stand.'

U khynnah u *ïeng* ha rúd lynti, The lad IS STANDING on the road-side.

Ïeng (transitive)=' to possess,' ' to guarantee.'

U Montri jong u sím hí *u'n ïeng* shi hajar tyngká, The king's chief adviser will himself guarantee 1000 Rs.

(3.) *Don* (intransitive)=' to be.'

Nga'm shym *don* hajan mynkata, I WAS not near at that time.

Don (transitive)=' to have,' ' to possess.'

U Saheb u *don* lai ngut ki khún, The gentleman HAS three children.

(4.) *sngow* (intransitive)=' to feel,' *or*, ' to be.'

Nga *sngowbhá* shibún eh, I am very much pleased.

U *sngow* suk shibún eh, He FEELS very happy.

Sngow (transitive)=' to hear.'

U tymen u'm *sngow* satïa ia phi, The old man DOES not HEAR you at all.

U kypá jong nga u *sngow*-pang dik-dik, My father FEELS acute pain.

Man has the meaning of ' to become.'

Ka samla ka'm *man* bhá satïa, The girl does not IMPROVE at all.

Or, like *mih*=' to yield,' *or*, ' to produce.'

Íh when compounded with an adjective or adverb; as,

íh-mat=' to be probable,' and ' to see.'

íh-sih=' to be ugly, hateful, &c.,' and ' to hate.'

íh-bein=' to be despicable,' and ' to despise.'

íh-bhá=' to be handsome,' and ' to take a fancy to.'

§ 202. The verbs *long* and *don*, ' to be.'

These two verbs are often confounded by foreigners. The distinction does not in all points correspond with that between হয় and আছে in Bengali. *Long* signifies existence, generally and absolutely, *don* simply ' to be ' under certain limited conditions; as,

U Blei U long, God is, *or*, God exists.

U Blei U don hangne, God IS here.

Uta u briw u shù long, That man exists merely.

Uta u briw u *don*, That man IS PRESENT.

In all descriptive phrases *long* signifies 'is,' but *don* never; as,

U Sím u *long* runar, The chief IS cruel.

U Sím u long bymman eh, The chief is very wicked.

Don in all such cases is inadmissible.

Long as bearing the meaning of 'to become,' is used of plants, for 'to take root;' of assemblies, for 'to take place;' as,

U symbai u'm long satïa, The seeds do not take root at all.

Ka dyrbar ka'm shym long, The council never took place.

Don signifies 'to have,' for ex. see § 201 (3).

Compare the following Bengali forms :—

ঈশ্বর হয়. শয়তান মন্দ হয়. ঈশ্বর এখানে আছেন, সে জন বাড়ীতে আছে. সে ব্যক্তির পীড়া আছে

THE PASSIVE VOICE.

§ 203. Read again § 67. . . . . . When the agent, or material, or the instrument with which an action is done, is expressed, it should be governed by *da* or *bad*.

1. *Present. Dang tháw ia ka íng,* The house is being built.

Sometimes the indefinite *ki* (they) is used as a nominative.

Ki dang tháw ia ka íng da ki ding, They are building the house with *or* of wood.

2. *Past. La tháw ia ka íng da ki ít,* The house was built of bricks.

La thoh ia ka shitti da U Jarkhá, The letter was written by U Jarka.

La lah pyniap ia ka massi da U Míet, The cow was killed by U Miet.

La dang lah pyniap ia ka massi, The cow had just been killed.

3. *Future. Yn tháw ia ka íng,* The house will be built.

Yn sa tháw íng, Houses will be built shortly.

Lano yn tháw ia ka íng? When will the house be built?

Lano yn thoh ia ka shitti? When will the letter be written?

Ynda la lah tháw ia kata ka íng, ngi'n die ia kane, After that house has been built, we will sell this one.

Haba dang lah-tháw ia kane ka íng, kumno yn thied ia kawei? When this house has just been built, how can another be bought?

PRESENT INDICATIVE.

§ 204. Continued state or action is expressed both by the simple verb, and by the particles *da*, *dang*, and *nang*; as,

U khynnah u trei minot bad la ki kot, The boy is working hard with his books.

U khynnah u *da* trei bad la ki kot, The boy is working with his books.

U khynnah u *dang* trei ha lyngkhá, The lad is (STILL) working in the field.

U khynnah u nang iáid sha shiwa ia ngi, The lad is going on before us.

Note.—*Da* is our English "ing;" *dang* and *nang* were originally adverbs; *dang* connects present action or state with the *past;* *nang* connects the present with the future; as mere tense auxiliaries. This distinction is important to notice.

§ 205. In *narration,* the present of *apodosis* expresses past time; as,

Mynba nga *don* hangta, u *da bhá* eh, When I WAS there, he WAS very good.

Haba ngi la ia shem bad u saheb, u *da kren* eh, When we met with the gentleman, he WAS SPEAKING harshly.

Hynda ngi la pyníh ia u, u'm *don* ei-ei ba'n ia thuh,

After we had explained to him, he HAD nothing to say.

Ha kaba lashái U Joan, u *ioh-íh* ia U Jísu, ba u wan, The next day, John SEETH Jesus coming, &c. John i. 29.

Ha kito ki sngi te, U *wan* U Joan, not *la wan;* In those days COMETH John, &c.

§ 206. In the active voice only, the *present* expresses future time, sometimes; as,

Nga wan pat, bad nga'n pyddiang ia phi, I am coming again, and I will receive you.

The Imperfect Tense.

§ 207. In narration the *past imperfect* is often expressed by the present with *da;* as,

U'nïang thliw u *da pyniap* bún briw mynwei, The small-pox USED TO KILL a great many formerly.

Ki shakri ki la iawan bad ki *da iarap* ia u, The servants came, and they WERE HELPING him.

Ha khymíh ki angel ki la wan bad ki *da iarap* ia u, Behold angels came, and they WERE HELPING him.

Matt. iv. 11 (see also Matt. xiii. 8, where the same construction would apply with more elegance).

§ 208. An inchoative act, that is, something commenced but not actually carried out, should be expressed by the past imperfect with *dang;* take, *e.g.*, Heb. xi. 17.

Uta uba la lah ioh ia ka jingkular, u la dang kinngia-noh ia la u khún, He that had received the promises, WAS OFFERING his own son, i.e. was in the very act of offering his son Isaac when the angel came to prevent him.

This distinction should be carefully observed, as it suggests at once to the native reader the true state of things under which Abraham acted, as well as the nature of his obedience to the Divine command. The first part of the verse says that he *had* offered his son, that is, in principle, and the latter part explains the apparent inconsistency "*that he was* (in the act of) *offering.*"

The Future.

§ 209. To the ordinary form with *yn* (will) the particle *sa* is added when certainty, or nearness of a future or contemplated action is to be expressed; as,

U'n *sa* wan khot ia phi, He will come to call you SOON.
U'n *sa* leit khet soh, He will SOON go to gather oranges.

But *sa* without *yn,* in narration, implies a close succession of events:

Ynda u la tháw ia la ka íng, u *sa* leit shong hí, After he has built his house, he will go to live there himself; *Or,* After he HAD finished his house, he went to live there himself.

The latter rendering is equally correct. It is with this particle of narration *sa* that the natives blunder so often and so inexcusably, when they always render the *future* form in Khassi by the future in English.

§ 210. The Future is used to express a command; as,

Phi'n leit shi syndon, Go at once.
Phi'n ym leit da lei-lei, Don't go by any means.

§ 211. The verb *leit* (to go) is used as an auxiliary to express what is about to take place, or likely to take place; not unlike μέλλω in Greek grammar, and *aller* or *va* in French.

U dang *leit* tháw íng, He is GOING to build a house.

Phi *leit* iáp noh, You WILL SURELY die.

§ 212. The *Future Perfect* is rarely used in compound sentences; as,

U *la lah pyndep* ia la ka kam la shai, He WILL HAVE finished his business to-morrow.

U'n la lah pyndep, &c., might be used as well.

Haba u'n poi hangne la shái, u *la lah ioh-íh* ia u, When he comes here to-morrow, he WILL HAVE SEEN him.

U'n la lah ioh-íh, &c., might be used.

§ 213. *Ynda*, usually translated 'when,' 'after,' is strictly a particle of the future tense, and, like *haba*, with a past tense gives the true *Future Perfect* in Khassi; as,

Ynda u la iáp, nga'n ioh bún spah, When he will have died, I will have much wealth.

This is evident from such sentences as the following:—

Nga'*n da la lah don* hangta, haba phi'n poi, I will have been there, when you shall arrive. For *Nga'n da*=*Nga yn da*. Also *Ynda khymih.*

Note.—Here lies the true distinction between *ynda* and *hynda*. The former refers to the future, and the latter to past time. Hence also the principal sentence following that introduced by *ynda* should always refer to the future.

The Past, Perfect, and Pluperfect.

§ 214. (1.) The form with *la*—the *past indefinite* or aorist has often the force of the *present* and *past complete*.

La wan u khynnah? U *la* wan, HAS the boy come? He HAS come.

Nga *la* thoh ia ka shitti, I HAVE written the letter.

Katba U *la* poi sha íng, ka la iap, As soon as he had arrived, she died.

(2.) The form with *la lah*—the *present complete* is used also for the *past complete.*

Nga la lah thoh ia ka shitti, I have written the letter. (*Present complete.*)

In compound sentences, having the accessory clause in the past, *la lah* is *past complete.*

Haba u la shong ha íng, ka shitti ka *la luh* poi, When he sat down in the house, the letter HAD ARRIVED.

The simple past in the principal clause would require another construction ; thus—

Mynba u shong ha íng, ka shitti ka *la poi,* When he was sitting in the house, the letter ARRIVED.

Interrogatives.

§ 215. Questions are indicated (1.) by means of particles, see § 198 ; or (2) by the tone of the voice.

(1.) We shall illustrate this rule by means of particles not exemplified under pronouns, such as *haei ?* where? *hangno ?* where? *shaei ?* where? *shano ?* where? *balei ?* why? *kumno ?* how? See § 82 *in extenso.*

Lano phi'n leit? When will you go?
U wan shane *balei ?* Why does he come here?
Ei ba kylli? Who is it that asks?
Kylli *mano ?* Who asks?
Kumno nga'n tip? How will I know?
Hato, kumno phi kren ia kata ka ktín? Pray, how do you speak so?

(2.) By the tone of the voice.

Phi'n leit noh *mynta?* Will you go away NOW?

Ka hukum ka long *pop?* Is the law SIN?

(3.) When an affirmative reply is expected, *mo* (is it not?) is added.

Phi'n wan pat la shái, *mo?* You will come back to-morrow, WILL YOU NOT?

Nga'n shem ia phi ha iew, *mo?* I will find you in the market, WON'T I?

(4.) But *mo* is also used ironically, to signify the extreme absurdity or improbability of what is apparently assented to in the question :—

Question. *Phi la kren bein ia u kypá jong nga,* You have spoken disparagingly of my father.

Answer. *Nga la kren bein ia u kypá jong phi mo?* I have spoken disparagingly of your father have I?

(5.) An affirmative reply is given by means of a negative question, thus :—

Phi'n wan? *Balei ym wan?* Will you come? WHY NOT?

Phi'm kloi? *Balei ym kloi?* Aren't you ready? WHY NOT?

(6.) A negative reply is given by means of an *affirmative* question :—

Ei ba shong hangne? Who lives here?

Nga'n leit tip shano? How can I know? I DON'T KNOW.

Phi leh býmman, You do wickedly.

Nga leh býmman *Mo?* I do wickedly DO I?

Of Negatives. (See § 65.)

§ 216. *Put* and *satïa* are used only with negative verbs, also *shym* (*with verbs in the past tense*).

U'm wan *satïa,* He never comes.

Nga'm tip *satïa,* I do not know AT ALL.

Ki'm *put* poi, They have not YET come.

Ki'm-put shym sngow, They have not YET heard.

Other particles are often used with negative verbs, but they are not necessarily and exclusively negatives as some have maintained, § 72:—

U'm wan *shuh,* He will not come AGAIN.

U'm tip *shuh,* He does not know AT ALL.

U'm *jiw* wan *shuh,* He NEVER comes AGAIN.

U'm *shym* wan *shuh,* He NEVER came again.

U'm *shym* shong *shuh,* He NEVER stopped ANY LONGER.

The Imperative.

§ 217. The particles of command are *tó, hó,* and *khíe* with *leit,* 'to go;' as,

Tó wan pat kloi sha la íng! Return home soon.

Tó leit kylli ia la u kypą́! Go and ask your father.

Tó pán bór na u sím ho! Ask permission from the chief, will you!

Kynriah ho! Stand on one side, will you!

Sngáp ho! Listen, *or*, Silence, will you!

Khie leit wád ia ka tyngká ho! Go for the money, will you!

Khie leit noh shi syndon ho! Be off at once, will you!

§ 218. In prohibitions *wat* (the Hin. مت) is employed, when the prohibition is strong, direct and decisive.

Wat wan shuh shane! Never come here again.

Wat put wan shane! Don't come here as yet.

Wat da kylli lushïa-eh katta, Don't be so inquisitive.

§ 219. Our English 'let' is expressed in Khassi by *ià* or *ái*, 'to give,' or *shah*, 'allow,' and *ieh*, 'let alone,' with the verb in the future; as,

Ià ngi'n ia leit noh! Let us be going!

Tó ái, ngi'n ia mih noh! Let us be away!

Tó shah, nga'n wan pat! Let me come back!

Tó ieh mynta! Let alone for the present!

§ 220. After *tó, khíe,* the present participle with *da* is often employed; as,

Tó khíe, da kylli bïang ho! Go, and ask again, will you!

Tó leit, da wád bïang ho! Go, and search again, will you!

Of the Moods and Tenses in Compound Sentences.

§ 221. Dependent clauses may form (1.) the subject of the principal verb; as,

Ba u la iap, ka long ka ba sngow sih shibún eh, That he is dead, is a very sad affair indeed.

Ba u'n leit noh, ka long kaba shisha hí, That he will go away, is true enough.

(2.) The object of the principal verb; as,

Nga tip, ba u la kham koit mynkata, I know that he was better then.

U la ioh-íh, ba u'm lah shuh pgndep (pres. for past), He saw, that he was not able to fulfil.

U la ioh íh, ba u'n ym lah pyndep shuh (fut.), He saw, that he would not be able to fulfil at all.

Nga la ioh-íh, ba u la khaweit shibún, I saw, that he was very much frightened.

U Sím u la lah ioh-sngow, ba phi pang eh, The chief had heard, that you are very ill.

U Syrdar u la tharai, ba phi'n da wan hi (future), The Sirdar thought that you would come yourself.

Sometimes the conjunctive *ba* is omitted; as,

U la tharai, phi'n wan hí, He thought, you would come yourself.

U la tharai, phi'n da la wan hí, He thought, you would have come yourself.

§ 222. Of conditional and dependent clauses, that is, such as are introduced by *lada*, 'if,' *la'*, 'though,' *haba*, 'if,' *ynda*, 'when' (fut.), *haba*, 'when' (past); we distinguish (*a*) *Those which suppose a fact.* These take the *present*, or *past indic.* in both members; as,

Lada u kren, nga jiw shah-shkór ia u, If he speaks, I always listen to him.

Lada u la kren shái, nga ruh nga la ioh sngow, If he spoke out, I also (must have) heard him.

(*b*) *Those which suppose a thing as possible or probable.* These take the future indic. in both clauses.

Lada u'n kren, nga ruh, nga'n shah shkór, If he will speak, I also, will listen.

Lada u'n ym kren, nga ruh nga'n ym kren, If he will or does not speak, I also will not speak.

(*c*) *Those which imply uncertainty.* These are introduced by *haba* and require the auxiliary of contingency *da* before the verb in the *future* in both members, the *Protasis* as well as *Apodosis*.

Haba u'n da kren shái, nga'n da tip kumno ba'n leh, Were he to speak out, I would know what to do.

Haba u'n da leh bhá, u kypa u'n da sngow suk, Were he to conduct himself properly, his father would feel happy.

(*d*) Those which imply that something has not been fulfilled or come to pass. These are introduced by *lada* with the *past perfect indicative* in the conditional clause or *protasis*, and the *future perfect* in the principal clause or *apodosis*.

Lada u la lah kren, nga'n ym da la lah konguh? If he had spoken, would I not have obeyed?

Lada u la lah konguh, nga'n da la lah ioh-sngow, If he had submitted, I would have heard.

This class will equally admit of the simple perfect in the principal clause or *apodosis*; thus,

Lada u la lah konguh, nga ruh nga la lah ioh-sngow, If he had submitted, I also would have heard.

Lada u la lah iap, phi'm shym la lah ioh-sngow ma-phi? If he were dead, would you not have heard?

Lada u la lah tháw íng hangta, nga'n ym da la lah leit shong da lei-lei sha Sohra, If he had built his house there, I would not have gone to Cherra to live on any account.

Lada u la lah leit noh, ka lah ba nga'n da la lah leit noh ma-nga hí ruh, If he had gone away, it is possible that I would have gone away myself as well; *or*, I might have gone, &c.

Lada u la leit noh, nga la pep noh, If he had gone, I would have remained.

Lada u la kren, nga la iathuh shisha ha phi, If he had spoken, I would certainly have told you.

(*e*) The force of the present tense in a subordinate clause will depend on the tense of the principal sentence; as,

U la lah wan thoh shitti mynba nga *ioh-ih* ia u. (Here the present *ioh-ih* should be rendered by a past tense, to correspond with the 1st clause.) He had been writing a letter when I SAW him.

On the force of *wan* in the above, see §§ 69, 225.

§ 223. Intentional clauses, or sentences expressing purpose, are introduced by *ba*, 'that,' 'in order that,' or by *khnang ba*, 'in order that;' as,

U la ong ia kata baroh, ba'n phi'n ioh tip, He said all that, in order that you may know.

U la ong ia kata baroh, khnang ba phi'n ioh tip, He said all that, in order that you may know.

U la ong ia kata baroh, ba phi'n *da ioh* tip, He said all that, that you MIGHT know.

U la ong ia kata baroh khnang ba phi'n *da ioh* tip, He said all that, in order that you MIGHT know.

Note.—For the force of *ioh*, see § 79.

The Infinitive.

§ 224. One verb governs another in the Infinitive Mood. The sign of the infinitive *ba'n* is often omitted; as,

U wan kylli bïang shaphang kata; U wan ba'n kylli bïang sh-kata, He comes to make further inquiries about that matter.

U kulai u dang hïar sha'wah ba'n dih ùm, The horse is just going down to the river, to drink.

U khynnah une, u wan pule kot, This lad is come to study. (Lit., to read books.)

U Syrdar u la leit ái dyrkhat, The Sirdar is gone to lodge a suit.

U nang thoh, or *U nang ba'n thoh,* He is able to write, *or* He can write.

U nang iaid, or *U nang ba'n iaid,* He is able to walk, *or* He can walk.

Note.—We have already explained under § 61 that *nang* is employed as an auxiliary of tense. In the above sentences it may be taken either as a principal verb (to be able) governing its infinitive, or as an auxiliary of mood (*potential*), He can, &c.

§ 225. We would here again refer the student to our remarks on *wan* ('to come') under § 69, as an auxiliary of tense in the *present perfect progressive.* This construction is analogous to, if not identical with, the French idiom with *Venir de,* lit., to come from.

French.—Il vient de batir une maison, He has (just) been building a house.

Khassi.—U la lah wan tháw íng, He has been building, &c.

U la lah wan tháw íng, mynba nga ioh-ih ia u, He had been building a house, when I saw him.

In this construction with *wan* the infinitive participle *ba'n* is not understood, that would give another meaning.

§ 226. The infinitive has only one, viz., the *present*

form, and its tense in any particular sentence is determined by that of the governing verb; thus,

Ka *dei* ia nga ba'n leit noh (present), I ought, *or* should go away.

Ka *la dei* ia nga ba'n leit noh (past), I ought to, *or*, should have gone away. (Lit., It was proper for me to go away.)

In some cases the English past infinitive cannot be rendered except by a dependent clause.

Ki ong ba u la leh ia kata shisha, He is said to have done that surely. Lit., They say, that he has done that, &c.)

Ki ngeit baroh, ba u la don ha iew mynta, lit., It is believed by all that he was in the market to-day. He is believed to have been in the market to-day.

§ 227. The infinitive (*with or without its object*) may be either the subject or the object of the principal verb; as,

Ba'n ngeit ia kata ka eh shibún (subject), To believe that is very difficult.

U la ong ia phi ba'n leit noh (object), He told you to go away.

U'n da sngowbhá ba'n pynngeit ia phi, He would like to persuade you.

§ 228. Our verbal noun in *ing* is formed by prefixing the feminine article *ka* to the (verbal) adjectives formed from verbs; thus, *bám*, *v.* to eat; *babám*, eating; *kaba bám*, to eat or the verbal noun 'eating,'=*ba'n bám*.

iám, *v.* to weep; *ba iám*, weeping.

u briw baiám, a weeping man (adjective).

kaba iám jong u briw, the weeping of the man (infinitive).

u briw babám, a voracious man.

kaba bám jong u briw, the man's eating.

In many cases the verb in its simple form will have the same meaning, but in others *euphony* demands the form with *kaba*.

Kaba pule kot ka pynshai ia ka mynsím, READING enlightens the mind.

But, U la wan *ia ka ba'n pule* kot, He came to read (purpose).

§ 229. The infinitive of purpose, or our gerundial infinitive is used in lieu of the form explained under § 223 (with *ba*) that is, the form *ia ka ba'n*; as,

Don bún íng *ia ka ba'n wái* shane, There are many houses FOR HIRE here.

U la khreh *ia ka ba'n ái* tyngka, He is prepared TO ADVANCE money.

U pynsngow-is'nei *da kaba iam*, He excites pity, by weeping.

The Participle.

§ 230. The present participle in *ing* differs from the infinitive in *ing* in that it *agrees* with a substantive like an adjective; for which reason it is sometimes called a *verbal adjective.*

The verbal adjective, or the participle in 'ing' in English, when employed (1.) as a *primary predicate* is expressed by prefixing *da* to the verb, with the article; as,

U iám, He weeps.	U *da* iám, He (is) WEEPING.
U thoh, He writes.	U *da* thoh, He (is) WRITING.
U la iám, He wept.	U *da* la iám, He was WEEPING.
U la thoh, He wrote.	U *da* la thoh, He was WRITING.

The particle *da* in this construction conveys the idea of simultaneity as well as relation to some other verb.

Ka dohnud jong ngi ka'm shym *da* la íng mo hapoh jong ngi? Was not our heart BURNING within us? Luke xxiv. 32.

(2.) But when this participle *in English* is a *secondary predicate,* or as an adjunct to the principal verb, *da* is prefixed *without* the article; as,

U la hikai ia ki, *da* ong, He (Jesus) taught them, SAYING, Matt. v. 2.

U la kren, *da iám,* He spoke, weeping.

U la leit noh da iám, He went away, weeping.

(3.) This is also rendered by prefixing *ia* to the verb used as an adjunct, or secondary predicate.

U khynnah u la wan *ia-phet,* The lad came RUNNING.

(4.) When employed as an attribute, *descriptive* or *causal*, is rendered by a subordinate clause in Khassi, introduced by an adverb ; as,

U Iakob *hamar ba u sa iap* u la kyrkhú ia la ki khún uwei-uwei-ruh, Heb. xi. 21, Jacob, DYING, blessed each of his sons.

U kypa, *ba u mut sniw*, u la phet noh, The father, SUSPECTING, escaped.

Note.—When these and other prepositions are used with the form *kaba*, such as *da kaba iám*, 'by weeping,' *na kaba sngowsih*, 'from grieving,' *ia ka ba'n thied*, 'for buying,' we have a true gerundial infinitive, expressing 'means,' 'purpose,' fitness,' &c.

Da kaba iai pynneh, phi'n hikai shen, BY PERSEVERING you will soon learn.

Da kaba kren shinna, phi'n pynngeit ia u, By speaking plainly, you will convince him.

§ 231. The English *perfect participle* (*as an attribute*) is rendered in Khassi either (1.) by the simple verb with the adverb *ynda*, 'after ;' as,

Ynda thoh la ka shitti, u la iám eh, HAVING WRITTEN his letter, he wept much.

Ynda khot ia nga sha la íng, u la síw baroh, HAVING CALLED me to his house, he paid all.

Or, (2.) by a subordinate clause introduced by *hynda*.

Hynda u la khot ia nga sha la íng, u la síw baroh.

Hynda u la thoh ia la ka shitti, u la iám eh.

§ 232. We here give a few examples of English sentences, with the *perfect participle* rendered into Khassi, as models to follow :—

(1.) I saw the letter WRITTEN, Nga la ioh-íh ia ka shitti, *hynda la thoh.*

(2.) I saw the letter BEING WRITTEN, Nga la ioh-íh ia ka shitti, *haba dang thoh.*

(3.) I heard the order BEING READ, Nga la ioh-sngow ia ka hukum *haba ki dang pule* ia ka.

(4.) The work DONE in this place is immense, Ka kam *ba la leh* shane ka long ka bakhráw eh.

(5.) The beasts SHOT this year are very few, Ki mrád *ba lasïat* ha kane ka snem ki khyndiat eh.

(6.) He saw the house BEING PAINTED, U la ioh-íh ia ka íng *haba ki dang niád rong* ia ka.

(7.) Whatsoever we have heard DONE at Cherra, do also here, Ia kaei-kaei-ruh ba ngi la ioh sngow *ba la leh* ha Sohra, leh kumjuh hangne.

CHAPTER VI.

Adverbs.

§ 233. For the usual position of the adverb, see § 98 and examples there given ; the following are exceptions to the general rule, *kham,* 'rather,' *shait,* 'briskly,' 'constantly,' *ksaw,* 'frequently,' *jiw,* 'ever,' *put,* 'yet,' *shym*, 'not.' Most of these were originally used as independent verbs, to govern the now principal verb in the infinitive, e.g. *jiw*, lit. means 'to be in the habit,' so *ksáw*, *shait*, 'to be strong,' 'to be fond of.'

U'm *jiw* wan, He never comes, lit., He is not USED to come.

U *jiw* leit, He makes a habit to go, = He is in the habit of going.

U *shait* bám doh, He is ALWAYS eating flesh meat.

U shait iám, He is ALWAYS crying.

U khlá u *ksáw* bám briw, The tiger OFTEN devours men.

U'm *shym* sngowthuh, He did NOT understand.

U sím u *kham* sngowsih, The chief is SOMEWHAT offended.

§ 234. By mere juxtaposition, a feature characteristic of the Turanian languages, most verbs and adjectives, and even nouns, are converted into adverbs; as,

U nongbylla u trei-*shitom*, The labourer works HARD.

U khynnah u hikai-*bhá*, The boy learns WELL.

U Saheb u ïáid-*mïan*, The gentleman walks SLOWLY.

U Mahajon u die-*duh*, The merchant sells AT A LOSS.

§ 235. Adverbs have degrees of comparison like adjectives.

U 'riw-líng u trei *kham minot* bad la ki jár, The boatman works MORE DILIGENTLY at his nets.

U 'riw-líng u trei *kham minot tam* bad ki jár, The boatman works MOST DILIGENTLY at the nets.

U 'riw-líng u trei minot tam eh bad ki jár, The boatman works MOST DILIGENTLY OF ALL with the nets.

CHAPTER VII.

Of Prepositions.

§ 236. Prepositions are distinguished from adverbs in that they govern nouns or their substitutes.

Ki iatrei *naduh* mynhynnin, They are working SINCE yesterday.

Nga'm tip ei-ei *shaphang* kata, I know nothing ABOUT that matter.

§ 237. Some prepositions, when they do not govern and stand alone, are adverbs.

Ka kypér ka don ar phew pruh *pynkïang*, The garden is twenty cubits broadways.

Ka íng ka la pyddang *sha neng*, The house is cracked above.

§ 238. The following prepositions require special notice:

(1.) *bad* (lit., and) 'with.'

Nga'n ia kren *bad* phi, I will speak WITH you.

(2.) *bad* used for *ia*, 'against.'

U ialeh *bad* nga, He fights WITH me.

(3.) *bad* to express the *material cause*, 'of.'

U la tei la ka íng *bad* u máw, He built his house with, *or* OF stone.

Da expresses the *instrumental* cause.

U nongbylla u la khet ia ka díng *da* ka sydi, The labourer cut down the tree WITH an axe.

U la tháw la ka íng *da* ka surkhi, He built his house WITH mortar.

La pyniap ia u snïang *da* i speh, The pig was killed WITH a pointed bamboo.

Na expresses the origin or source *from* which.

Kane ka kam ka long *na* ka jingshún suda, This business arises entirely from enmity.

U la síw *na* lade, He paid FROM his own pocket.

Sha, 'to,' that is 'motion to.'

Nga'n leit *sha* shnong, I will go TO the village.

Ha, 'in,' or 'at,' and sometimes 'to' and 'with.'

Me'n shong *ha* íng, Thou wilt stay AT home.

U la ái ia ka kitab *ha* phi, He gave you the book.

Ka kitab ka don *ha* nga, The book is WITH me.

U la buh ia ka dud *ha* íng, He put the milk IN THE house.

Note.—Sha is used by natives where we would expect *ha*, but then the relative position of the speaker is taken into consideration.

U shong *sha* la íng, He sits IN his house.

U'm don *sha* shnong, He is not IN the village.

Ia, 'to,' 'for,' 'against,' implies direct and immediate relation. Hence its being the sign of the dative and of the accusative case as well.

U la ái ia ka kitab *ia* nga (see ex. under *ha*), He gave the book TO me, *that is*, to be MINE.

To pynkren *ia* nga ho? Speak FOR me, will you?

§ 239. After verbs of giving, promising, speaking, &c., *ia* implies that what is given, said, &c., is in the interest of, or about, the person addressed.

U la kren eh ia phi, He spoke harshly OF you.

U la kular ia nga ia kata, He promised me that.

Ha in these instances would imply only a local relation.

U la kren *ha* nga,=He spoke TO, *and not* OF, me.

§ 240. *Jong* is very probably the same as the abstract *jing*, both denoting possession. In some districts *jing* is used instead of *jong* as a particle of possession.

Jing nga for *jong nga*=of me=my.

CHAPTER VIII.

Of Conjunctions.

§ 241. *Bad*, 'and,' either connects words and clauses following in succession or separated from each other by the principal verb; as,

(1.) *Ki la die-noh ia ka íng bad ki jingbuh*, They sold the house and the furniture.

(2.) *U Saheb bad ka mem ki la ia wan-kái*, The gentleman and his wife came for a walk.

Note.—In these examples the words connected are *co-ordinate.*

(1.) *U Saheb u la wan-kái, bad ka mem de*, The gentleman came for a walk, WITH his lady.

(2.) *Ka íng ka la íng-duh-noh, bad ki jingbuh*, The house went on fire, and the furniture.

Note.—Here *bad* merely adds a second particular to the main *object of the sentence.*

§ 242. *Ruh, de*, and *ruh de* are post-positive conjunctions. They differ from *bad* in the same way that 'and' and 'also' are to be distinguished.

U Miet u la pyniáp ia ka massi, *bad* u sniang *ruh*, Miet killed the cow, and the pig ALSO.

Nga'n leit khymíh ia u kypá jong phi lashái, bad u para *ruh de*, I will go to see your father to-morrow, and your brother ALSO.

Hermann's rule on the Greek τε . . . καὶ applies to *bad* and *ruh*, &c., that *bad* connects ideas, while *ruh* and *de* merely add some subordinate idea.

(2.) But *ruh* (lit., also, too) has the force of our 'even.'

Nga'm shym kren shikyntín *ruh*, I did not say one word EVEN.

Ba'n ang la ka shintur *ruh*, ym núd, One dares not open his mouth EVEN.

Bad haduh mynta *ruh*, u'm put la ieh noh, And up to the present EVEN, he has not left (it) off.

(3.) *Wad*, 'even,' is used *prepositively*, either alone or with *ruh*.

Wad haduh mynta *ruh*, u'm put ieh noh, EVEN up to the present, he has not left (it) off.

(4.) *Hinrei*, 'but,' *pynban*, 'yet,' 'notwithstanding,' *putet*, 'nevertheless,' are used post-positively sometimes.

Nga'm jiw la don hangta *hinrei*, BUT, I have never been there, *or*, I never was there.

This is a mode of giving an emphatic denial or contradiction.

Nga la sngáp jar, u sngowsih *pynban*, I kept silent; he is offended NOTWITHSTANDING.

U la ong ba phi'n ym wan; phi la wan *pynban*, He told you not to come; YET you have come.

§ 243. 'Both . . . and' are expressed by *bad* . . . *bad;* as,

Ngi la ioh-íh ia u, bad ma-nga bad ma-phi, Both I and you, saw him.

Ngi la thíed baroh, bad íng bad jingbuh, We bought all, both house and furniture.

§ 244. *Ba*, 'that,' has various functions.

(1.) To introduce apposition and object clauses.

Ka long kaba shisha hí, ba u la duh tyngka, It is quite true, that he has lost money.

Nga tip eh, ba phi la duh tyngka, I know well that you have lost money.

(2.) To express purpose; as,

U leit sha Labun ba u'n ioh kren bad u kyngi, He goes to Shillong, that he may speak with his his uncle.

Note.—Khnang, 'purposely,' is often used before *ba*; thus,

U leit khnang bad u'n ioh ia kren badu kypa.
U leit khnang ba'n ioh ia kren bad u kypa.

(3.) To express the cause or reason of an action; as,

U phah shim dawái ba-pang eh u khún, He sends for medicine, because his child is very ill.

Ba u'm tip kumno ba'n leh, nga'n leit lem, Since he does not know how to proceed, I will go with him.

§ 245. Certain prepositions and adverbs used conjunctively take *ba,* such as *naduh, haduh, namar, hamar.*

U'n ieit ia mé haduh b'ynda iáp; or, *haduh ba u'n da iáp,* He will love thee, TILL death.

U'n íh-síh ia me ha b'ynda iáp, He will hate you till death.

Naduh ba phi wan, ym don ba kren bad nga, SINCE you have come, no one speaks with me.

U'm kren shuh, *namar ba* phi la ái dyrkhat, He never speaks, BECAUSE you have lodged a suit.

La die-noh ia ka massi, *hamar ba* phi dang ia-kren, The cow was sold whilst you were talking together.

Na ka bynta ba phi'n 'riwbhá, u kypá u'm put die ia ka bri, In order to make you rich, your father has not yet sold the grove.

§ 246. 'Though . . . yet' are rendered by *la . . . pynban.*

La' phi'm ïeit shibún ia nga, phi la iarap *pynban,* Though you do not love me much, yet you have helped me.

'Whether . . . or' by *la'* . . . *lane.*

La' ka long ma-nga *lane* ma-phi, phi'n wan kumjuh, WHETHER it is me OR you, you will come all the same.

La' phi'n leit *ne* ém, ka'm iaphér ei-ei, Whether you go or not, it makes no difference whatever.

'As . . . so' by *kumba . . . kumta,* or *kumba . . . kumjuh.*

Kumba phi bet kumta phi'n òt, As you sow, so must you reap.

'Not only . . . but also' by *ym tang . . . hinrei ruh.*

Ka kypér ka'*m* long *tang* ka ba íh-tynnad *hinrei* ka ba don kam ruh, The garden is NOT ONLY beautiful, BUT useful.

Uta u briw u long *ym tang* u bastád, *hinrei* u ba bhá ruh, That man is NOT ONLY learned, BUT ALSO good.

'So . . . that' by *katta . . . ba.*

Nga'm long u basníw katta ba nga'n leit tuh, I am not so bad THAT I would go and pilfer.

§ 247. 'Neither . . . nor,' as a *strengthened* negative, is rendered by *lymne . . . lymne.*

U'm shym ong ei-ei, *lymne* ia kaba bhá *lymne* ia kaba sníw, He said nothing, NEITHER good NOR bad.

'Neither . . . nor' is rendered by *lane . . . lane,* with *ym.*

Nga'm íhthuh, *lane* ia phi *lane* ia u, I do not know either you or him, = I know NEITHER you NOR him.

'Either . . . or' is rendered by *lane* alone or *lane . . . lane.*

Yn ioh ka bri u Narain lane ka para jong u, Either Narain or his sister will have the grove.

Lane ma-nga lane ma phi yn ioh ia ka bri, Either I or you will have the grove.

§ 248. *Ia* when used as a conjunction signifies 'than'; as,

U kypá jong nga u kham khráw *ia* nga, My father is greater than I.—John.

Sometimes *ba'n* is prefixed; thus,

U Sím u la ái kham bun ia nga, ba'n ia phi, The chief gave me more THAN (he gave) to you.

Ba'n ia kane, bhá kato, That is better THAN this, lit., THAN this good that.

Ba'n ia kaba'n leit shatai, kham bhá ba'n shong shane, RATHER THAN go there, it is better to stay here.

CHAPTER IX.

The Interjections.

§ 249. *Ynnai dei* is often used for "What's the use!"

Phi'n shim ia une u soh? Ynnai phi! Will you take these oranges? What's the use!

Ieh, 'Let alone!' 'Leave it there!'

To thíed ia kane ka jain shi tyngka. Ieh! Buy this cloth (for) a rupee. No, leave it there.

ERRATA.

Page 5, line 2, *after* 'and' *read* 'is.'

Page 6, line 2, *for* থা *read* ঋ